Dr. Dobson Answers Your Questions

Marriage

D0628214

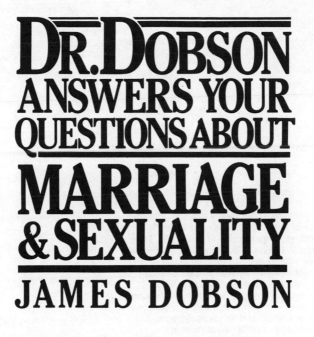

DR. DOBSON
ANSWERS YOUR QUESTIONS ABOUT
MARRIAGE & SEXUALITY

JAMES DOBSON

TYNDALE HOUSE PUBLISHERS, INC., WHEATON, ILLINOIS

ACKNOWLEDGMENTS

It is with gratitude that I hereby acknowledge the assistance of four women who contributed significantly to the production of this book. They are *Virginia Muir*, Senior Editor at Tyndale House Publishers, who assembled original material from my prior writings and recordings; *Dee Otte*, my Administrative Assistant, who kept the wheels turning when they would otherwise have ground to a halt; *Teresa Kvisler*, who typed and collated the final manuscript; and, of course, my beloved wife, *Shirley*, who is an active partner in everything I do. Without the encouragement and dedication of these four members of the "team," a half finished manuscript would remain hopelessly buried beneath a mountain of paper on my desk.

Dr. Dobson Answers Your Questions about Marriage and Sexuality is selections from *Dr. Dobson Answers Your Questions,* copyright © 1982 by James C. Dobson, published by Tyndale House Publishers, Inc.

Excerpts from *Hide or Seek* by Dr. James Dobson, copyright © 1974, 1979, published by Fleming H. Revell Company, Old Tappan, NJ 07675, used by permission.

Excerpts from *Preparing for Adolescence* by Dr. James Dobson, copyright © 1978, published by Vision House Publishers, Santa Ana, CA 92705, used by permission.

Excerpts from *Straight Talk to Men and Their Wives* by Dr. James Dobson, copyright © 1980, published by Word Books, Waco, TX 76796, used by permission.

First printing, November 1986
Library of Congress Catalog Card Number 86-50760
ISBN 0-8423-0622-6

This book is affectionately dedicated to the professional colleagues and staff members who help me direct the activities of our nonprofit ministry, Focus on the Family. Paul Nelson, Gil Moegerle, Peb Jackson, Rolf Zettersten, Mike Trout, and 360 other coworkers and friends are deeply devoted to the principles and values expressed throughout this book.

It is entirely appropriate, therefore, that I take this opportunity to thank them for their diligent efforts to preserve the institution of the family.

A Word from the Publisher

Who is Dr. James Dobson and why is
he offering advice, herewith, on
family-related subjects ranging from
toddlerhood to television and from
sibling rivalry to sex education?
That question must be answered at
the outset on behalf of those
individuals who have neither read
his books, seen his films, heard his
radio program, viewed his television
broadcasts, nor listened to his
cassette tape recordings. If you find
yourself in that dwindling number,
perhaps we can best introduce you
to the work of James Dobson
through the following article
published originally in the *Saturday
Evening Post,* April 1982, and
written by Charles W. Phillips.

(Factual information in this article, such as
the ages of the Dobson children and the
number of radio stations that carry his
broadcast, has been updated.)

FOCUS ON THE FAMILY

Author James Dobson calls upon his deeply ingrained Judeo-Christian values to connect the family of the '80s with the principles of "discipline, love, self-esteem, loyalty and fidelity."

CHARLES W. PHILLIPS

Credit a man with eight best-selling books, give him a radio show on 900 stations, put him in a film series to be viewed by 50 million people and book him on shows with Donahue and Tom Snyder and that same man is an instant celebrity . . . a full-fledged personality. Unless his name is Dr. James Dobson.

A tall, handsome man who is both dignified and downhome, tough but sympathetic, Dobson only recently is achieving fame beyond Christian circles. Thanks to a swing back to conservatism, his family-first philosophy is suddenly in vogue, his traditional values are suddenly acceptable, his ideas are suddenly in season.

Depending on who's counting, Dobson wears at least seven—no, make that eight—hats. Sometimes, in the course of a day he switches from one to another so smoothly, so adroitly, so often, that he might add quick-change artist to the list of vocations separated by commas after the Ph.D. in his name. Answering to the labels of father, husband, associate clinical professor of pediatrics at the University of Southern California School of Medicine, psychologist, author, radio and TV personality and speaker, Dobson manages a balancing act in the Flying Wallenda tradition. The trick, he has learned, is to maintain priorities and never let one role dominate at the expense of the others. At this, too, he succeeds.

The immensity of his influence in the areas of child and family psychology has been likened to that of Dr. Benjamin Spock of twenty years ago, although the similarity ends there. Dobson is a politically conservative, back-to-basics disciplinarian who believes in spoiling the rod to spare the child and who practices at home what he preaches on film, in books and around the lecture circuit.

"First and foremost, I'm a committed Christian," he explains. "I was raised in a Christian home, and those values are ingrained deeply within me. Most of what I teach is an outgrowth of traditional Christian concepts with regard to the family and home. I get a great deal of satisfaction in feeling used by God in the lives of people. I don't find my work stressful at all; in fact, I'm having the time of my life. The most difficult aspect is trying to keep it all under control and not let my professional identity interfere with my roles as father and husband."

It was this inevitable tug between his private and professional lives that helped convince him in 1979 to put his Focus on the Family seminar on tape. The seminar, usually offered in person by Dobson over a one-day or two-day period, centers on such topics as Christian fathering, preparing for adolescence, building self-esteem and the conflict of wills between parent and child. When the film idea was first presented by Word Publishers of Waco, Texas, he argued that surely no one would sit through seven one-hour films and watch a man stand in front of an audience and talk about traditional values and discipline. Reluctantly, he agreed to the project and admits today that his worst fears have been proven "dead wrong."

"The film series was actually a method of coping with so many demands on my time," he recalls. "I was getting anywhere from 500 to 1,000 speaking requests a year and was accepting about six per month. That might not sound like much until you realize most talks and seminars take place on weekends. Put that way, I wasn't with my children enough. I began to feel I was losing out on something. The films allowed me to stay home and yet get the message out."

The tapes, usually shown over a seven-week period or in succession over seven days, not only had immediate impact but have shown staying power. Marketing executives at Word say some 50 million people have already viewed the films at a clip of 100,000 persons per week. Most of the screenings are at local churches—more than 50,000 at latest count—but a variety of other organizations, including members of NFL teams, PTAs and military installation personnel, also have viewed them.

The format of the films is simple. In the fall of 1978, Dobson was scheduled to deliver his much-in-demand Focus on the Family seminar to 3,000 persons jammed into Laurie

Auditorium in San Antonio. Special guests included wife Shirley, mother Myrtle and a film crew assigned to videotape the entire Friday night and all-day Saturday sessions. Except for the opening sequences and a few closeups of the audience, the films' visual content is limited to Dobson at the podium or occasionally at the large onstage chalkboard. Surprisingly, each of the one-hour segments passes quickly, thanks to Dobson's well-documented research, relaxed delivery and frequent anecdotes. He draws on his experience as the father of a twenty-year-old daughter and fifteen-year-old son and his years as associate clinical professor of pediatrics at the University of Southern California School of Medicine. He recalls his daughter's first slumber party, when he, as an observer, quickly recognized the popularity pecking order of the girls in attendance. Using such memories as a base, he spins off into discussions of peer pressure and the importance of having a positive self-image. Recollections of his son's "terrible twos" serve as a springboard for talks about headstrong toddlers and strong-willed adolescents.

"If I have a motive in what I'm doing, it's nothing more ambitious than to connect the family in the '80s with the wisdom of the Judeo-Christian ethic—the traditional wisdom that's been with us for thousands of years," he explains. "The principles haven't changed, and they still work. I'm referring to discipline, love, self-esteem, loyalty and fidelity between husband and wife and commitment within the family. These aren't new ideas; I've never said I created anything new. That's why I have confidence in what I'm saying, because I didn't originate it—it existed long before I was born. All I've attempted to do is to take the wisdom that's been with us for thousands of years and put it in a package that people find interesting and entertaining. Hopefully, it captures their imagination and provides the motivation to do what they probably already knew was right."

Part of the interesting, entertaining package is the Dobson family itself. Although Dobson stoutly occupies the role of lone breadwinner and protective head of the household, he's hardly a throwback to the Neanderthal man who demanded submission and dragged the little woman around by her topknot. Dobson's done his share of diapering and dishes and marvels at wife Shirley, a former teacher, for her easy superiority at the art of homemaking. Their relationship is a solid, warm partnership based on respect.

"We've been married twenty-five years, and she is literally my best friend. If I had one evening to spend with any personality on earth, I'd spend it with Shirley. We have a great deal in common, and it's a testimonial to the power of love that I could be with anybody for twenty-five years and still find that person interesting, but she affects me that way."

Although his lectures are amply sprinkled with descriptive tales from the Dobson family archives, he's careful to stop short of relocating Shirley, Danae and Ryan from their comfortably private California home to life in a fishbowl. He discovered the danger of overexposure one weekend when Ryan accompanied him to a speaking engagement and was pressed for an autograph. The bewildered five-year-old responded, "But I can't even write." From that point onward, the subject of Dad's work has been low-keyed at home. The children seldom listen to his radio broadcasts (now aired thirty minutes daily on 900 stations), rarely watch him on television and are not preoccupied with the flourishing ministry that attracts some 6,200 letters to his office each day.

In spite of his image as Superdad, he feels no undue pressure to rear two perfect, "textbook" children. Observers might look to the Dobsons as model parents with model offspring, but Dobson draws a more realistic picture.

"My kids are healthy, seemingly happy and get along well in school. But these principles I teach don't need Danae and Ryan to prove them valid. They'll be valid even if I fail as a father. They existed before I came along, and they'll be here after I leave. God doesn't need me to prove what he said about the family is right. Even if everything goes to pieces at my house—and I pray it doesn't—the principles will still be true."

And they'll be true fifty years from now, long after the era of permissiveness, the "me" generation and the do-your-own-thing life style have gone the route of other fads, believes Dobson. The pendulum has swung back to traditional values, he says, and although the family unit is in real trouble, luckily, people recognize the threat, are looking for answers and are hungry for the kind of self-help information he provides.

"The most dangerous threat to family life is one seldom mentioned," says Dobson. "We can talk about alcoholism, drug abuse or infidelity, but a more common threat is the simple matter of overcommitment. I'm talking about the husband and wife who are too exhausted to take walks together, understand one another, meet each other's needs, have time for play, have time for children, have time for devotions. The husband often moonlights to maintain some standard of living; the wife works and tries to oversee the home; everyone is on the brink of exhaustion. I see that as the quickest route to the destruction of the family, and it can happen so easily.

"Sure, we have to make a living, but there's more to overcommitment than that. Why do we have to have a standard of living that we didn't have thirty years ago? I think we're sacrificing things that are absolutely irreplaceable. Things like relationship with the family, the loving interaction between husband and wife, parent and child. When you lie on your deathbed and look back over your life, you won't remember the new automobile, the new couch or the neighborhood you lived in. You'll remember who loved you, who cared for you and where you fit into somebody's life. If those things matter then, they should matter now, and we ought to live like they do."

Some people might find dealing with other families' problems discouraging, but Dobson sees it as fulfilling. He's a man of principle and those principles are the heart of his message.

"They work when people live by them rather than allowing their own needs to dominate everyone else in the family. At one point, people were taught to scream for their rights. This is disastrous when it's applied to the national level. What works best is when I say to you, 'I care about you as much as I care about myself. Your needs are my needs.' That's what makes life worth living. It's not when I clench my fists and grit my teeth and set out to get my own way."

Dobson's way is quieter, and it's winning converts every time he presents his case on a talk show, at a seminar, through a film or another book.

"I find it tremendously exciting to have an opportunity to express creativity in figuring out where people's needs are and where the hurts are and how to help them. I don't see myself as a crusader trying to change the world by myself, but I can do what I can. I can do my part."

Reprinted with permission from *The Saturday Evening Post* Society, a division of the Benjamin Franklin Literary and Medical Society, Inc., ©1982. From the April 1982 issue.

CONTENTS

SECTION 1
ROMANTIC LOVE

Do you believe love at first sight occurs between some people?

Though some readers will disagree with me, love at first sight is a physical and emotional impossibility. Why? Because love is not simply a feeling of romantic excitement; it is more than a desire to marry a potential partner; it goes beyond intense sexual attraction; it exceeds the thrill at having "captured" a highly desirable social prize. These are emotions that are unleashed at first sight, but they *do not constitute love.*

Real love, in contrast to popular notions, is an expression of the deepest appreciation for another human being; it is an intense awareness of his or her needs and longings—past, present, and future. It is unselfish and giving and caring. And believe me, these are not attitudes one "falls" into at first sight, as though we were tumbling into a ditch.

I have developed a lifelong love for my wife, but it was not something I fell into. I *grew* into it, and that process took time. I had to know her before I could appreciate the depth and stability of her character—to become acquainted with the nuances of her personality, which I now cherish. The familiarity from which love has blossomed simply could not be generated on "Some enchanted evening, across a crowded room." One cannot love an unknown object, regardless of how attractive or sexy or nubile it is![1]

Do you believe real love can easily be distinguished from infatuation?

No, I do not. I must stress this fact with the greatest emphasis:

The exhilaration of infatuation feels like love at its best, but it is *never* a permanent condition. Period! If you expect to live on the top of that mountain, year after year, you can forget it! Emotions swing from high to low to high in cyclical rhythm, and since romantic excitement is an emotion, it too will certainly oscillate.

How, then, can real love be distinguished from temporary infatuation? If the feeling is unreliable, how can one assess the commitment of his will? There is only one answer to those questions: It takes time. The best advice I can give a couple contemplating marriage (or any other important decision) is this: make *no* important, life-shaping decisions quickly or impulsively, and when in doubt, stall for time. That's not a bad suggestion for all of us to apply.[2]

Do you believe that God selects one particular person for each Christian to marry and He relentlessly brings them together?
No, and that is a dangerous supposition to rely on. A young man whom I was counseling once told me that he awoke in the middle of the night with the strong impression that God wanted him to marry a young lady whom he had only dated casually a few times. They were not even going together at that time and hardly knew each other. The next morning he called her and relayed the message which God had supposedly sent him during the night. The girl figured she shouldn't argue with God, and she accepted the proposal. They have now been married for seven years and have struggled for survival since their wedding day!

Anyone who believes that God preempts free choice and thereby guarantees a successful marriage to every Christian is in for a shock. This is not to say the He is disinterested in the choice of a mate, or that He will not answer a specific request for guidance on this all-important decision. Certainly, His will should be sought in such a critical matter, and I consulted Him repeatedly before proposing to my wife. However, I do not believe that God performs a routine match-making service for everyone who worships Him. He has given us judgment, common sense, and discretionary powers, and He expects us to exercise these abilities in matters matrimonial. Those who believe otherwise are likely to enter marriage glibly, thinking, "God would have stopped us if He didn't approve." That is a dangerous posture to assume on so important a decision.[3]

Do you believe that genuine love between a husband and wife is permanent, lasting a lifetime?
It can be, and indeed, should be. However, even genuine love is a fragile flower. It must be maintained and protected if it is to survive. Love can perish when a husband works seven days a week . . . when there is no time for romantic activity . . . when he and his wife forget how to talk to each other. The keen edge on a loving relationship may be dulled through the routine pressures of living. Where does your marriage rank on your hierarchy of values? Does it get the leftovers and scraps from your busy schedule, or is it something of great worth to be preserved and supported? It can die if left untended.[4]

I am a nineteen-year-old girl and I'm still single. I'm aware of some pretty awful circumstances that can occur in marriage. If that's the way it is, why should I bother to get married at all?
Coping with a bad marriage can be a terrible experience, I'll grant you, but a good marriage is a lifelong treasure. I can tell you from a personal point of view that my marriage to Shirley is the best thing that ever happened to me, and there are millions who can offer a similar testimony. You see, life involves problems no matter what your choices are; if you remain single, your frustrations will be of a different nature but they will occur, nevertheless. As to whether you should get married or not, I would offer you the same advice given me when I was an eight-year-old child, by a Sunday school teacher whose name I don't even remember: He said, "Don't marry the person you think you can live with; marry the person you think you can't live without . . . if such an individual ever comes along." Either way, I think you're ahead by knowing in advance that married life offers no panacea—that if it is going to reach its potential, it will require an all-out investment by both husband and wife.[5]

Do you think happily married husbands and wives should be able to live together without fighting with one another?
No. The healthiest marriages are those where the couple has learned *how* to fight—how to ventilate anger without tearing one another apart. I'm saying that there is a difference between healthy and unhealthy combat, depending on the way the

disagreement is handled. In an unstable marriage, the hostility is usually hurled directly at the personhood of the partner: "You never do anything right; why did I ever marry you? You are incredibly dumb and you're getting more like your mother every day." These personal comments strike at the heart of one's self-worth and produce an internal upheaval. Obviously, such vicious combat is extremely damaging to a marital relationship. Healthy conflict, on the other hand, remains focused on the issue around which the disagreement began: "You are spending money faster than I can earn it!" "It upsets me when you don't tell me you'll be late for dinner." "I was embarrassed when you made me look foolish at the party last night." These areas of struggle, though admittedly emotional and tense, are much less damaging to the egos of the opposing forces. A healthy couple can work through them by compromise and negotiations with few imbedded barbs to pluck out the following morning.

The ability to fight *properly* may be the most important concept to be learned by newlyweds. Those who never comprehend the technique are usually left with two alternatives: (1) turn the anger and resentment inward in silence, where it will fester and accumulate through the years, or (2) blast away at the personhood of one's mate. The divorce courts are well represented by couples in both categories.[6]

SECTION 2

CONFLICT IN MARRIAGE

What is *the* most common marital problem you hear about in your office?

Let's suppose I have a counseling appointment at four o'clock tomorrow afternoon with a person whom I've never met. Who is that person and what will be the complaint that brings them to me? First, the patient will probably be Mrs. Jones, not her husband. A man is seldom the first to seek marriage counseling, and when he does, it is for a different motive than his wife seeks it. She comes because her marriage is driving her crazy. He comes because his *wife* is driving him crazy.

Mrs. Jones will be, perhaps, between twenty-eight and forty-two years of age, and her problem will be *extremely* familiar to me. Though the details will vary, the frustration she communicates on that afternoon will conform to a well-worn pattern. It will sound something like this:

> John and I were deeply in love when we got married. We struggled during the first two or three years, especially with financial problems, but I knew he loved me and he knew I loved him. But then something began to change. I'm not sure how to describe it. He received a promotion about five years ago, and that required him to work longer hours. We needed the money, so we didn't mind the extra time he was putting in. But it never stopped. Now he comes home late every evening. He's so tired I can actually hear his feet dragging as he approaches the porch. I look forward to his coming home all day 'cause I have so much to tell him, but he doesn't feel much like talking. So I fix his dinner and he eats it alone. (I usually eat with the kids earlier in the evening.) After dinner, John makes a few phone

calls and works at his desk. Frankly, I like for him to talk on the telephone just so I can hear his voice. Then he watches television for a couple of hours and goes to bed. Except on Tuesday night he plays basketball and sometimes he has a meeting at the office. Every Saturday morning he plays golf with three of his friends. Then on Sunday we are in church most of the day. Believe me, there are times when we go for a month or two without having a real, in-depth conversation. You know what I mean? And I get so lonely in the house with three kids climbing all over me. There aren't even any women in our neigborhood I can talk to, because most of them have gone back to work. But there are other irritations about John. He rarely takes me out to dinner and he forgot our anniversary last month, and I honestly don't believe he's ever had a romantic thought. He wouldn't know a rose from a carnation, and his Christmas cards are signed, just "John." There's no closeness or warmth between us, yet he wants to have sex with me at the end of the day. There we are, lying in bed, having had no communication between us in weeks. He hasn't tried to be sweet or understanding or tender, yet he expects me to become passionate and responsive to him. I'll tell you, I can't do it. Sure, I go along with my duties as a wife, but I sure don't get anything out of it. And after the two-minute trip is over and John is asleep, I lie there resenting him and feeling like a cheap prostitute. Can you believe that? I feel used for having sex with my own husband! Boy, does that depress me! In fact, I've been awfully depressed lately. My self-esteem is rock bottom right now. I feel like nobody loves me . . . I'm a lousy mother and a terrible wife. Sometimes I think that God probably doesn't love me, either. Well, now I'd better tell you what's been going on between John and me more recently. We've been arguing a lot. I mean really fighting. It's the only way I can get his attention, I guess. We had an incredible battle last week in front of the kids. It was awful. Tears. Screaming. Insults. Everything. I spent two nights at my mother's house. Now, all I can think about is getting a divorce so I can escape. John doesn't love me anyway, so what difference would it make? I guess that's why I came to see you. I want to know if I'll be doing the right thing to call it quits.

Mrs. Jones speaks as though she were the only woman in the world who has ever experienced this pattern of needs. But she is

not alone. It is my guess that 90 percent of the divorces that
occur each year involve at least some of the elements she
described—an extremely busy husband who is in love with his
work and who tends to be somewhat insensitive, unromantic,
and noncommunicative, married to a lonely, vulnerable, romantic woman who has severe doubts about her worth as a human
being. They become a matched team: he works like a horse and
she nags.[1]

**My husband is somewhat insensitive to my needs, but I
believe he is willing to do better if I can teach him how I
am different from him. Can you help me communicate my
needs to him effectively?**
First, let me tell you how *not* to handle this assignment. Do not
resort to what I have called the "bludgeoning technique," which
includes an endless barrage of nagging, pleading, scolding,
complaining, and accusing. This is how that approach sounds
to an exhausted man who has come home from work moments
before: "Won't you just put down that newspaper, George, and
give me five minutes of your time? Five minutes—is that too
much to ask? You never seem to care about my feelings, anyway. How long has it been since we went out for dinner? Even if
we did, you'd probably take the newspaper along with you. I'll
tell you, George, sometimes I think you don't care about me and
the kids anymore. If just once . . . just once . . . you would show a
little love and understanding, I would drop dead from sheer
shock," etc., etc., etc.
   Obviously, that is not the way to get George's attention. It's
like pounding him behind the ear with a two-by-four, and it
rarely achieves more than a snarl when he gets up from the
floor. Instead, you should look for opportunities to teach your
husband during moments of closeness and understanding.
That instruction requires the proper timing, setting, and manner to be effective.
   1. *Timing.* Select a moment when your husband is typically
more responsive and pleasant; perhaps that opportunity will
occur immediately after the evening meal, or when the light
goes out at night, or in the freshness of the morning. The worst
time of the day is during the first sixty minutes after he arrives
home from work, yet this is the usual combat hour. Don't lum-
ber into such a heavy debate without giving it proper planning
and forethought, taking advantage of every opportunity for the
success of the effort.

2. *Setting.* The ideal situation is to ask your husband to take you on an overnight or weekend trip to a pleasant area. If financial considerations will cause him to decline, save the money out of household funds or other resources. If it is impossible to get away, the next best alternative is to obtain a baby-sitter and go out to breakfast or dinner alone. If that too is out of the question, then select a time at home when the children are occupied and the phone can be taken off the hook. Generally speaking, however, the farther you can get him from home, with its cares and problems and stresses, the better will be your chance to achieve genuine communication.

3. *Manner.* It is extremely important that your husband does not view your conversation as a personal attack. We are all equipped with emotional defenses which rise to our aid when we are being vilified. Don't trigger those defensive mechanisms. Instead, your manner should be as warm, loving, and supportive as possible under the circumstances. Let it be known that you are attempting to interpret *your* needs and desires, not *his* inadequacies and shortcomings. Furthermore, you must take his emotional state into consideration, as well. Postpone the conversation if he is under unusual stress from his work, or if he isn't feeling well, or if he has recently been stung by circumstances and events. Then when the timing, setting, and manner converge to produce a moment of opportunity, express your deep feelings as effectively as possible. And like every good boy scout: be *prepared.*[2]

Are you suggesting that a woman should crawl on her belly like a subservient puppy, begging her master for a pat on the head?

Certainly not! It is of the highest priority to maintain a distinct element of dignity and self-respect *throughout* the husband-wife relationship. This takes us into an area that requires the greatest emphasis. I have observed that many (if not most) marriages suffer from a failure to recognize a universal characteristic of human nature. *We value that which we are fortunate to get; we discredit that with which we are stuck! We lust for the very thing which is beyond our grasp; we disdain that same item when it becomes a permanent possession.* No toy is ever as much fun to play with as it appeared to a wide-eyed child in a store. Seldom does an expensive automobile provide the satisfaction anticipated by the man who dreamed of its ownership. This principle is even more dramatically accurate in romantic affairs, particularly with reference to men.

Let's look at the extreme case of a Don Juan, the perpetual lover who romps from one feminine flower to another. His heart throbs and pants after the elusive princess who drops her glass slipper as she flees. Every ounce of energy is focused on her capture. However, the intensity of his desire is dependent on her unavailability. The moment his passionate dreams materialize, he begins to ask himself, "Is this what I really want?" Farther down the line, as the relationship progresses toward the routine circumstances of everyday life, he is attracted by new princesses and begins to wonder how he can escape the older model.

Now, I would not imply that all men, or even the majority of them, are as exploitative and impermanent as the gadabout I described. But to a lesser degree, most men *and* women are impelled by the same urges. How many times have I seen a bored, tired relationship become a torrent of desire and longing the moment one partner rejects the other and walks out. After years of apathy, the "dumpee" suddenly burns with romantic desire and desperate hope.

This principle hits even closer to home for me at this moment. Right now, as I am writing these words, I am sitting in the waiting room of a large hospital while my wife is undergoing major abdominal surgery. I am writing to ease my tension and anxiety. While I have always been close to Shirley, my appreciation and tender love for her are maximal this morning. Less than five minutes ago, a surgeon emerged from the operating room with a grim face, informing the man near me that his wife is consumed with cancer. He spoke in unguarded terms of the unfavorable pathological report and the malignant infestation. I will be speaking to Shirley's surgeon within the hour and my vulnerability is keenly felt. While my love for my wife has *never* flagged through our fourteen years together, it has rarely been as intense as in this moment of threat. You see, not only are our emotions affected by the challenge of pursuit, but also by the possibility of irrevocable loss. (The surgeon arrived as I was writing the sentence above, saying my wife came through the operation with no complications, and the pathologist recognized no abnormal tissue. I am indeed a grateful man! My deepest sympathy is with the less fortunate family whose tragedy I witnessed today.)

Forgive the redundancy, but I must restate the principle: *we crave that which we can't attain, but we disrespect that which we can't escape.* This axiom is particularly relevant in romantic matters, and has probably influenced *your* love life, too. Now, the forgotten part of this characteristic is that marriage does not erase or change it. Whenever one marriage partner grovels in his own disrespect . . . when he reveals his fear of rejection by his mate . . . when he begs and pleads for a handout . . . he often faces a bewildering attitude of disdain from the one he needs and loves. Just as in the premarital relationship, nothing douses more water on a romantic flame than for one partner to fling himself emotionally on the other, accepting disrespect in stride. He says in effect, "No matter how badly you treat me, I'll still be here at your feet, because I can't survive without you." That is the best way I know to kill a beautiful friendship.

So what am I recommending . . . that husbands and wives scratch and claw each other to show their independence? No! That they play a sneaky cat and mouse game to recreate a "challenge"? Not at all! I am merely suggesting that self-respect and dignity be maintained in the relationship.[3]

I'm certain that I'm losing my husband. He shows signs of boredom and total disinterest in me. He treats me rudely in public and is virtually silent at home. And of course, our sex life is non-existent. I have begged and pleaded with him to love me, but I'm losing ground every day. What can I do to save my marriage?
These are symptoms of a condition which I call "the trapped syndrome." More often than not, the man is thinking these kinds of thoughts: "I'm thirty-five years old" (or whatever age) "and I'm not getting any younger. Do I really want to spend the rest of my life with this one woman? I'm bored with her and there are others who interest me more. But there's no way out 'cause I'm stuck." These are the feelings which usually precede esoteric infidelity, and they certainly can be felt in the strain between a husband and wife.

How should a woman respond when she reads the cues and realizes that her husband feels trapped? Obviously, the worst thing she could do is reinforce the cage around him, yet that is likely to be her initial reaction. As she thinks about how important he is to her, and what-on-earth she would do without him, and whether he's involved with another woman, her anxiety may compel her to grab and hold him. Her begging and pleading only continue to drive him to disrespect her more, and the relationship continues to splinter. There is a better way which I have found productive in counseling experience. The most successful approach to bringing a partner back toward the center of a relationship is not to follow when he moves away from it. Instead of saying, "Why do you do me this way?" and "Why won't you talk to me?" and "Why don't you care anymore?" a wife should pull back a few inches herself. When she passes her husband in the hall and would ordinarily touch him or seek his attention, she should move by him without notice. Silence by him is greeted by silence in return. She should not be hostile or aggressive, ready to explode when he finally asks her to say what is on her mind. Rather, she responds in kind . . . being quietly confident, independent, and mysterious. The effect of this behavior is to open the door on his trap. Instead of clamping herself to his neck like a blood-sucking leech, she releases her grip and introduces a certain challenge in his mind, as well. He may begin to wonder if he has gone too far and may be losing something precious to him. If that will not turn him around, then the relationship is stone, cold dead.

What I am recommending to you is extremely difficult to express in written form, and I am certain to be misinterpreted by some of my readers on this issue. I haven't suggested that you rise up in anger—that you stamp your feet and demand your domestic rights, or that you sulk and pout in silence. Please do not associate me with those contemporary voices which are mobilizing feminine troops for all-out sexual combat. Nothing is less attractive to me than an angry woman who is determined to grab her share, one way or the other. No, the answer is not found in hostile aggression, but in quiet self-respect!

In short, personal dignity in a marriage is maintained the same way it was produced during the dating days. The attitude should be, "I love you and am totally committed to you, but I only control my half of the relationship. I can't demand your love in return. You came to me of your free will when we agreed to marry. No one forced us together. That same free will is necessary to keep our love alive. If you choose to walk away from me, I will be crushed and hurt beyond description, because I have withheld nothing of myself. Nevertheless, I will let you go and ultimately I will survive. I couldn't demand your affection in the beginning, and I can only request it now."

Somehow, that releasing of the door on the trap often results in revolutionary changes in a relationship.[4]

As much as I love my wife (and I'm convinced she loves me), our relationship has become stagnant in recent years. It seems like all we do is work—clean house, take care of the kids, fix the leaking roof, have the car repaired, etc.—you know, trying to keep up with the routine responsibilities of living. How can we escape this deadening lifestyle? How can we liven up our marriage?
You have described a situation which I call the "straight life," referring to the never-ending responsibilities of adult living that become oppressive and deadening to a marriage. To let it continue unchanged is to sacrifice something precious in your relationship. I suggest you make a conscious effort to put four new ingredients back into your lives, beginning with pleasure. You and your wife should go on a date at least once a week, leaving children at home. Likewise, some form of sports or recreational activity should be enjoyed as a family, whether it be tennis, golf, swimming, skiing, or another option.

Second, you should seek to keep the romantic fires aglow in your relationship, by the use of love notes and surprises and candlelight dinners and unexpected weekend trips, among other possibilities.

Third, you *must* reserve some of your time and energy for meaningful sexual activity. Tired bodies make for tired sex. The physical aspect of the relationship can be approached creatively, and indeed, must be.

Fourth, the most successful marriages are those where both husband and wife seek to build the self-esteem of the other. Ego needs *can* be met within the bonds of marriage, and nothing contributes more to closeness and stability than to convey respect for the personhood of the spouse.

Every responsible adult must cope with the concerns of the straight life, but those obligations need not assault mental and physical health and marital harmony.[5]

I've concluded that my husband *cannot* comprehend my emotional needs. He will not read books that I give him, nor will he attend seminars, listen to tapes, or even talk to me about my frustrations. Nevertheless, he is a good man who is faithful to me and has been an effective father. What do you suggest I do with this dilemma?
The answer I'm about to give you will *not* satisfy you. But I know it is consistent with the will of God. My advice is that you

change that which can be altered, explain that which can be understood, teach that which can be learned, revise that which can be improved, resolve that which can be settled, and negotiate that which is open to compromise. Create the best marriage possible from the raw materials brought by two imperfect human beings with two distinctly unique personalities. *But for all the rough edges which can never be smoothed and the faults which can never be eradicated, try to develop the best possible perspective on the difficulty and determine in your mind to accept reality exactly as it is.* The first principle of mental health is to accept that which cannot be changed. You could easily go to pieces over the adverse circumstances beyond your control, but you can also resolve to withstand them. You can *will* to remain stable, or you can yield to cowardice.

Someone wrote:

> Life can't give me joy and peace;
>   it's up to me to *will* it.
> Life just gives me time and space;
>   it's up to me to fill it.

Can you accept the fact that your husband will *never* be able to meet all your needs and aspirations? Seldom does one human being satisfy every longing and hope in the breast of another. Obviously, this coin has two sides: You can't be his perfect woman, either. He is no more equipped to resolve your entire package of emotional needs than you are to become his sexual dream machine every twenty-four hours. Both partners have to settle for human foibles and faults and irritability and fatigue and occasional nighttime "headaches." A good marriage is not one where perfection reigns; it is a relationship where a healthy perspective overlooks a multitude of "unresolvables." Thank goodness my wife, Shirley, has adopted that attitude toward me![6]

You mentioned the term "perspective" twice in the previous answer. Explain what you mean by it.
Let me say it another way. A slight revision in your perception of your husband can make him appear much more noble. The gifted author (and my friend) Joyce Landorf has explained this perspective better than anyone I've heard. During the early years of her marriage, she found herself angry at her husband for dozens of reasons. Dick inadvertently conveyed insults to

her by his manner and personality. For example, just before retiring each evening, he would say, "Joyce, did you lock the back door?" She always answered affirmatively, whereupon Dick walked to the door to verify that it was bolted. There were only two ways for Joyce to interpret his behavior. Either he thought she was lying about the door, or else he didn't think she had the brains to remember locking it. Both alternatives made her furious. This scenario symbolized many other sources of conflict between them.

Then one night as Dick proceeded to check the lock, the Lord spoke to Joyce.

"Take a good look at him, Joyce," He said.

"What do you mean, Lord?" she replied.

"I have made your husband a door checker. He's a detail man. That's why he's such a good banker. He can examine a list of figures and instantly locate an error that others have overlooked. I gave him that ability to handle banking responsibilities. Yes, Joyce, I made Dick a 'door checker,' and I want you to accept him that way."

What a fantastic insight. Many times a man's most irritating characteristic is a by-product of the quality his wife most respects. Perhaps his frugality and stinginess, which she hates, have made him successful in business, which she greatly admires. Or perhaps his attentiveness to his mother's needs, which his wife resents, is another dimension of his devotion to his own family. Or, maybe his cool stability in the face of crisis, which drew his wife to him, is related to his lack of spontaneity and exuberance during their tranquil days. The point is, *God gave your husband the temperament he wears, and you must accept those characteristics that he cannot change. After all, he must do the same for you.* This is what I meant when I said I *knew* it is God's will for us to persevere. He wants us to be tough—to see this life as temporary and not all that important: The Apostle Paul expressed this mental toughness best as he sat in jail, writing to his Christian friends. He said,

> For I have learned, in whatsoever state I am, therewith to be content. I know both how to be abased, and I know how to abound: every where and in all things I am instructed both to be full and to be hungry, both to abound and to suffer need. I can do all things through Christ which strengtheneth me (Phil. 4:11-13 KJV).[7]

I must admit that my husband is also unable to meet my needs. He's an unromantic, noncommunicative man who will *always* be like that. The impasse is set in concrete. Rather than persevere, as you suggested, I've been thinking about getting a divorce. But I'm reluctant to do it and am continually "arguing" with myself over whether to bail out or not. Tell me, is divorce the answer for people like me?

How often I have seen women go through the agitation you describe. Such a person contemplates this alternative of divorce day and night, weighing the many disadvantages against the one major attraction: *escape.* She worries about the effect of separation on the kids and wonders how she'll be able to support them and wishes she didn't have to tell her parents. Round and round go the positives and negatives. Should I or shouldn't I? She is both attracted and repelled by the idea of a dissolution.

This contemplative stage reminds me of a classic documentary film which was shot during the earliest days of motion pictures. The cameraman captured a dramatic event that took place on the Eiffel Tower. There, near the top, was a naive "inventor" who had constructed a set of bird-like wings. He had strapped them to his arms for the purpose of using them to fly, but he wasn't totally convinced that they would work. The film shows him going to the rail and looking downward, then pacing back and forth. Next he stood on the rail trying to get enough courage to jump, then returned to the platform. Even with the primitive camera of those days, the film has captured the internal struggle of that would-be-flier. "Should I or shouldn't I? If the wings work, I'll be famous. If they fail, I'll fall to my death." What a gamble!

The man finally climbed on the rail, turned loose of the nearby beam, and wobbled back and forth for a breathless moment of destiny. Then he jumped. The last scene was shot with the camera pointed straight downward, as the man fell like a rock. He didn't even bother to flap his wings on his way to the ground.

In some respects, the depressed homemaker is like the man on the ledge. She knows that divorce is a dangerous and unpredictable leap, but perhaps she will soar with the freedom of a bird. Does she have the courage to jump? No, she'd better stay on the safety of the platform. On the other hand, this could be the long-sought escape. After all, everyone else is doing it. She wavers momentarily in confusion . . . and often takes the plunge.

But what happens to her then? It's been my observation that her "wings" do not deliver the promised support. After the wrenching legal maneuvers and custody fight and property settlement, life returns to a monotonous routine. And what a routine. She has to get a job to maintain a home, but her marketable skills are few. She can be a waitress or a receptionist or a sales lady. But by the time she pays a baby-sitter (*if* she can find one) there is little money left for luxuries. Her energy level is in even shorter supply. She comes home exhausted to face the pressing needs of her kids, who irritate her. It's a rugged experience.

Then she looks at her ex-husband who is coping much better. He earns more money than she and the absence of kids provides him more freedom. Furthermore (and this is an important point), in our society there is infinitely more status in being a divorced man than a divorced woman. He often finds another lover who is younger and more attractive than his first wife. Jealousy burns within the mind of the divorcee, who is lonely and, not surprisingly, depressed again.

This is no trumped-up story just to discourage divorce. It is a characteristic pattern. I've observed that many women who seek divorce for the same reasons indicated (as opposed to infidelity) will live to regret their decision. Their husbands whose good qualities eventually come into view, begin to look somewhat attractive again. But these women have stepped off the ledge . . . and they must yield to the forces of nature.

Divorce is not the answer to the problem of busy husbands and lonely wives. Just because the secular world has liberalized its attitudes toward the impermanence of marriage, no such revision has occurred in the biblical standard. Would you like to know *precisely* what God thinks of divorce? He has made His view abundantly clear in Malachi 2:13-17, especially with reference to husbands who seek a new sexual plaything:

> Yet you cover the altar with your tears because the Lord doesn't pay attention to your offerings anymore, and you receive no blessing from him. "Why has God abandoned us?" you cry. I'll tell you why; it is because the Lord has seen your treachery in divorcing your wives who have been faithful to you through the years, the companions you promised to care for and keep. You were united to your wife

by the Lord. In God's wise plan, when you married, the two of you became one person in his sight. And what does he want? Godly children from your union. Therefore guard your passions! Keep faith with the wife of your youth.

For the Lord, the God of Israel, says he hates divorce and cruel men. Therefore control your passions—let there be no divorcing of your wives.

You have wearied the Lord with your words.

"Wearied him?" you ask in fake surprise. "How have we wearied him?"

By saying that evil is good, that it pleases the Lord! Or by saying that God won't punish us—he doesn't care (TLB).[8]

Why are men so insensitive to women's needs today? They seem oblivious to the longings of their wives, even when every effort is made to communicate and educate.
I question whether men have really changed all that much over the years. Rather, I doubt if men have *ever* responded as women preferred. Did the farmer of a century ago come in from the fields and say, "Tell me how it went with the kids today"? No, he was as oblivious to his wife's nature as husbands are today. What has changed is the *relationship between women!*

A century ago women cooked together, canned together, washed clothes at the creek together, prayed together, went through menopause together, and grew old together. And when a baby was born, aunts and grandmothers and neighbors were there to show the new mother how to diaper and feed and discipline. Great emotional support was provided in this feminine contact. A woman was never really alone.

Alas, the situation is very different today. The extended family has disappeared, depriving the wife of that source of security and fellowship. Her mother lives in New Jersey and her sister is in Texas. Furthermore, American families move every three or four years, preventing any long-term friendships from developing among neighbors. And there's another factor that is seldom admitted: American women tend to be economically competitive and suspicious of one another. Many would not even consider inviting a group of friends to the house until it was repainted, refurnished, or redecorated. As someone said, "We're working so hard to have beautiful homes and there's nobody in them!" The result is isolation—or should I say insulation—and its first cousin: loneliness.[9]

I'm beginning to recognize a "blind spot" in my attitude toward my wife. I have always felt that I had done my job as a husband if I provided adequately for my family's financial needs and if I was faithful to Anita. But are you saying that I am also responsible to help meet her emotional needs, too?

That's right, especially today when homemakers are under such attack. Everything they have been taught from earliest childhood is being subjected to ridicule and scorn. Hardly a day passes when the traditional values of the Judeo-Christian heritage are not blatantly mocked and undermined.

- The notion that motherhood is a worthwhile investment of a woman's time suffers unrelenting bombardment.
- The concept that a man and woman should become one flesh, finding their identity in each other rather than as separate and competing individuals, is said to be intolerably insulting to women.
- The belief that divorce is an unacceptable alternative has been abandoned by practically everybody. (Have you heard about Sue and Bob?)
- The description of the ideal wife and mother, as offered in Proverbs 31:10-31 is now unthinkable for the modern woman. (She's come a long way, baby.)
- The role of the female as help-mate, bread-baker, wound-patcher, love giver, home builder, and child-bearer is nothing short of disgusting.

All of these deeply ingrained values, which many of today's homemakers are trying desperately to sustain, are continually exposed to the wrath of hell itself. The Western media—radio, television and the press—are working relentlessly to shred the last vestiges of Christian tradition. And the women who believe in that spiritual heritage are virtually hanging by their thumbs! They are made to feel stupid and old-fashioned and unfulfilled, and in many cases, their self-esteem is suffering irreparable damage. They are fighting a sweeping social movement with very little support from anyone.

Let me say it more directly. For the man who appreciates the willingness of his wife to stand against the tide of public opinion—staying at home in her empty neighborhood in the exclusive company of jelly-faced toddlers and strong-willed adolescents—it is about time her husband gave her some help. I'm not merely suggesting that he wash the dishes or sweep the floor. I'm referring to the provision of emotional support . . . of conversation . . . of making her feel like a lady . . . of building her ego . . . of giving her one day of recreation each week . . . of taking her out to dinner . . . of telling her that he loves her. Without these armaments, she is left defenseless against the foes of the family—the foes of *his* family![10]

What effect does this breakdown in the relationship between women have on marriages?

It can be devastating. Depriving a woman of all meaningful emotional support from outside the home puts enormous pressure on the husband-wife relationship. The man then becomes her primary source of conversation, ventilation, fellowship, and love. But she's not his only responsibility. He is faced with great pressure, both internal and external, in his job. His self-esteem hangs on the way he handles his business, and the status of the entire family depends on his success. By the time he gets home at night, he has little left with which to prop up his lonely wife . . . even if he understands her.

Let me speak plainly to the homemaker with a busy but non-communicative husband: *you cannot depend on this man to satisfy all your needs.* You will be continually frustrated by his failure to deliver. Instead, you must achieve a network of women friends with whom you can talk, laugh, gripe, dream, and recreate. There are thousands of wives and mothers around you who have the same needs and experience. They'll be looking for you as you begin your search for them. Get into exercise classes, group hobbies, church activities, Bible studies, bicycle clubs— whatever. But at all costs, resist the temptation to pull into the four walls of a house, sitting on the pity pot and waiting for your man to come home on his white horse.[11]

SECTION 3
THE HOMEMAKER

**As a homemaker, I resent the fact that my role as a wife
and mother is no longer respected as it was in my
mother's time. What forces have brought about this
change in attitudes in the Western world?**
Female sex-role identity has become a major target for change
by those who wish to revolutionize the relationship between
men and women. The women's movement and the media have
been remarkably successful in altering the way females "see"
themselves at home and in society. In the process, every element of the traditional concept of femininity has been
discredited and scorned, especially those responsibilities associated with homemaking and motherhood. Thus, in a period of a
single decade, the term *housewife* has become a pathetic sym-
bol of exploitation, oppression, and—pardon the insult—
stupidity, at least as viewed from the perspective of radical feminists. We can make no greater mistake as a nation than to
continue this pervasive disrespect shown to women who have
devoted their lives to the welfare of their families.[1]

**You mentioned the role of the media in this changing con-
cept of femininity. Are you implying that network
television and movie producers have *deliberately*
attempted to destroy or change the traditional role
played by American women?**
There is no doubt in my mind about that fact. The entertain-
ment industry has worked tirelessly to create a totally new
woman with remarkable capacities. We saw her during the sev-
enties as Wonder Woman and the Bionic Woman and Spider

Woman and Charlie's Angels and a host of other powerful (but sexy) females. In my book, *What Wives Wish Their Husbands Knew About Women*, I described this new socially prescribed role as follows:

> This image of women now being depicted is a ridiculous combination of wide-eyed fantasy and feminist propaganda. Today's woman is always shown as gorgeous, of course, but she is more—much more. She roars around the countryside in a racy sports car, while her male companion sits on the other side of the front seat anxiously biting his nails. She exudes self-confidence from the very tips of her fingers, and for good reason: she could dismantle any man alive with her karate chops and flying kicks to the teeth. She is deadly accurate with a pistol and she plays tennis (or football) like a pro. She speaks in perfectly organized sentences, as though her spontaneous remarks were being planned and written by a team of tiny English professors sitting in the back of her pretty head. She is a sexual gourmet, to be sure, but she wouldn't be caught dead in a wedding ceremony. She has the grand good fortune of being perpetually young and she never becomes ill, nor does she ever make a mistake or appear foolish. In short, she is virtually omniscient, except for a curious inability to do anything traditionally feminine, such as cook, sew, or raise children. Truly, today's screen heroine is a remarkable specimen, standing proud and uncompromising, with wide stance and hands on her hips.[2]

But she is unreal—just as phony as the masculine superheroes played by Burt Reynolds and Roger Moore. It is sheer fantasy on either side of the line of gender.[3]

What has been the result of this revolution in feminine sex-role identity and where is it likely to lead us from here?

It has produced a decade of depression and self-doubt among women. God created us as sexual beings, and any confusion in that understanding is devastating to the self-concept. Those most affected are the women who are inextricably identified with the traditional role, those who perceive themselves to be "stranded" in a homemaking responsibility. Thus, wives and mothers have found themselves wondering, "Who am I?" and then nervously asking, "Who *should* I be?" It appears that we tore down the old value system before the new one was ready for occupancy, bringing widespread confusion and agitation.

Now a new and surprising phenomenon is taking place. The self-doubt has spread to the masculine gender. I suppose it was inevitable. Any social movement creating chaos in half the population was certain to afflict the other half, sooner or later. As a result, men are now entering the winter of their discontent.

Psychology Today published an article by James Levine in which he reviewed three new books on the subject of manhood in transition. His opening paragraph is indicative of their content:

> After countless books about the condition of women that have been published in the last decade, we are now getting a spate of studies about men. *One theme comes through loud and clear: the male is in crisis.* Buffeted by the women's movement, constrained by a traditional and internalized definition of "masculinity," men literally don't know who they are, what women want from them, or even what they want from themselves (November 1979).

It's true. Men *are* in a state of confusion over the meaning of sex-role identity. We know it is unacceptable to be "macho" (whatever in the world that is), but we're a little uncertain about how a real man behaves. Is he a breadwinner and a protector of his family? Well, not exactly. Should he assume a position of leadership and authority at home? Not if he's married to a woman who's had her "consciousness raised." Should he open doors for his wife or give a lady his seat on the train or rise when she enters the room? Who knows? Will he march off to defend his homeland in times of war, or will his wife be the one to fight on foreign soil? Should he wear jewelry and satin shoes or carry a purse? Alas, is there anything that marks him as different from his female counterpart? Not to hear the media tell it!

Again, I must make the point that this confused sex-role identity is not the result of random social evolution. It is a product of deliberate efforts to discredit the traditional role of manliness by those who seek *revolution* within the family. Notice that James Levine referred to traditional masculinity as *constraining*. That is precisely how the liberal media and humanistic behavioral scientists perceive the biblical concept of maleness.[4]

**Are you saying that we should all be locked into tradi-
tional male and female sex roles, whether we choose them
or not? Are you telling every woman that she must bear
children even if she doesn't want them?**
Of course not. It is a woman's prerogative not to have a baby, so I
would not be so foolish as to try to force that decision on anyone.
However, there's something ambiguous about insisting on a
"right" which would mean the end of the human race if univer-
sally applied! If women wearied of childbearing for a mere
thirty-five years on earth, the last generation of mortals would
grow old and die, leaving no offspring to reproduce. What god-
like power is possessed by the female of the species! She can
take the bit in her mouth and gallop down the road to oblivion
with a wagonload of humanity bumping along behind. No
hydrogen bomb could destroy us more effectively, without
bloodshed or pollution.

But this is not merely a bad dream with no basis in reality. For
several years, it has been almost impossible to find anything
positive written about human babies in liberal and leftist publications. Kids have been perceived as an imposition, a nuisance,
and a drain on the world's natural resources. They're seen as
part of the "population bomb" that supposedly plagues the
earth. I'm convinced that this negative bias plays a role in the
epidemic of child abuse that rages throughout this country. It is
certainly related to the shameful abortion phenomenon occurring during the past decade. More than a million American
babies are now aborted annually (55 million worldwide), infants
who will never take their place in the fabric of our society. What
remains is an aging population with fewer children to step into
our shoes.

What I'm saying is that sex-role attitudes are closely related to
the survival of a society. What will happen, for example, if the
present generation reaches retirement age and still outnumbers
the younger workers? Who would support the social security
system when today's adults become too old to earn a living?
Who would populate the military when America is threatened
from abroad? What would happen to an economy that is based
on decreasing returns rather than growth from productivity?
Yes, the liberated woman will have had her way—her "right" to
abortion and childlessness. She will have proved that no one
could tell her what to do with her body. But what a victory![5]

What answer do you have for those who say being a mother and a housewife is boring and monotonous?
They are right—but we should recognize that practically every other occupation is boring, too. How exciting is the work of a telephone operator who plugs and unplugs switchboard connections all day long—or a medical pathologist who examines microscopic slides and bacterial cultures from morning to night—or a dentist who spends his lifetime drilling and filling, drilling and filling—or an attorney who reads dusty books in a secluded library—or an author who writes page after page after page? Few of us enjoy heart-thumping excitement each moment of our professional lives. On a trip to Washington, D.C., a few years ago, my hotel room was located next to the room of a famous cellist who was in the city to give a classical concert that evening. I could hear him through the walls as he practiced hour after hour. He did not play beautiful symphonic renditions; he repeated scales and runs and exercises, over and over and over. This practice began early in the morning (believe me!) and continued until the time of his concert. As he strolled on stage that evening, I'm sure many individuals in the audience thought to themselves, "What a glamorous life!" Some glamor! I happen to know that he had spent the entire day in his lonely hotel room in the company of his cello. Musical instruments, as you know, are terrible conversationalists. No, I doubt if the job of a housewife and mother is much more boring than most other jobs, particularly if the woman refuses to be isolated from adult contact. But as far as importance of the assignment is concerned, *no* job can compete with the responsibility of shaping and molding a new human being.

May I remind mothers of one more important consideration: you will not always be saddled with the responsibility you now hold. Your children will be with you for a few brief years and the obligations you now shoulder will be nothing more than dim memories. Enjoy every moment of these days—even the difficult times—and indulge yourself in the satisfaction of having done an essential job right!

How do you feel about mothers being employed outside the home, especially in situations where it is not financially necessary for her to work?
Editor's note: This question is of such significance and controversy in the Western world today, that it cannot be answered

with a brief reply. Therefore, the decision was made to reprint an article written by Dr. Dobson in which he addressed the matter of full-time employment for women.

WORKING MOTHERS AND THEIR FAMILIES

America is currently witnessing an unprecedented movement of women into the work force. More than half the 84 million adult females in this country are now formally employed; one in every three mothers of children under six is working outside the home, and the numbers are steadily rising. Whether or not this trend is healthy or pathological is one of the most volatile issues of our time, and one which generates heated debates and considerable conflict. Alas, everyone seems to have an opinion on the subject. You're about to read mine.

It would be presumptuous for any family specialist, particularly a man, to tell the women of America how to live their lives. The decision to have a career or be a homemaker is an intensely personal choice that can only be made by a woman and her husband. Indeed, the search for employment is often required by the inflationary pressures of today's economy. And there are marital disruptions where the husband either cannot work or is removed from the home. These and related problems obviously demand the financial contribution of the women involved. Thus, when a Christian wife and mother concludes that she must enter the labor force, the response from her friends and associates should be one of tolerance and understanding.

I must honestly report my observation, however, that working wives and their families often face some special frustrations and problems. Getting a job, especially for the mother of small children, can produce a whole catalog of new challenges which she may not comprehend in the beginning. In fact, I am concerned about the untruthful messages often given to the mother who can choose whether to work or stay home. Specifically, there are three false concepts being energetically conveyed to her through various forms of feminist propaganda. Let me consider them individually.

1. Every female in America who isn't "working" is being cheated and exploited by the male-dominated society in which she lives. If she has any gumption or intelligence, she'll seek fulfillment in a career.

Since the beginning of human existence, women in most cultures have identified themselves with child rearing and nest building. It was an honorable occupation that required no apology. How has it happened, then, that homemaking has fallen on such lean times in the Western world? Why do women who remain at home in the company of little children feel such disrespect from the society in which they live? A partial answer to these questions can be found in the incessant bombardment by the media on all traditional Judeo-Christian values.

Accordingly, it would appear that many women have accepted employment as a means of coping with the disrespect that they experienced as full-time mothers. To understand this process, let's look at a contrived example.

Suppose it suddenly became very unpopular to be a dentist. Suppose every magazine carried an article or two about the stupidity of the tooth-and-gum boys, making them look foolish and gauche. Suppose television commercials and dramas and comedy programs all poked fun at the same battered target. Suppose the humor associated with dentistry then died, leaving contempt and general disrespect in its place. Suppose the men in white were ignored at social gatherings and their wives were excluded from "in" group activities. Suppose dentists had difficulty hiring assistants and associates because no one wanted his friends to know he was working for a "tooth fairy." What would happen if all social status were suddenly drained from the profession of dentistry? I suspect that it would soon become very difficult to get a cavity drilled and filled.

The illustration is extreme, admittedly, but the analogy to women can hardly be missed. Housewives have been teased and ridiculed and disrespected. They have been the butt of jokes and sordid humor until the subject is no longer funny. As I have spoken to family groups across the country, great frustration has been expressed by women who have been made to feel dumb and foolish for wanting to stay at home. Those who are dedicated to their responsibilities are currently being mocked in women's magazines as "Supermoms." They have heard the prevailing opinion: "There must be something wrong with those strange creatures who seem to like domestic duties and responsibilities."

Closely related to the myth that "homemakers are losers" is a similar distortion related to child rearing.

2. Children, even those under five years of age, don't really need the extensive nurturing and involvement of their mothers, anyway. They will become more independent and assertive if raised in various child-care settings.

If the above statement were accurate, it would conveniently expunge all guilt from the consciences of overcommitted parents. But it simply won't square with scientific knowledge. I attended a national conference on child development held in Miami, Florida, a few years ago. Virtually every report of research presented during that three-day meeting ended with the same conclusion: the mother-child relationship is absolutely vital to healthy development of children. The final speaker of the conference was Dr. Urie Bronfenbrenner, the foremost authority on child development today. He concluded his remarks by saying that feminine responsibilities are so vital to the next generation that the future of our nation actually depends on how we "see" our women. I agree.

Nevertheless, modern women are struggling to convince themselves that state-sponsored child-care centers offer a convenient substitute for the traditional family concept. It will not work! It hasn't succeeded in the countries where it has been tried. As Dr. Bronfenbrenner wrote:

> . . . with the withdrawal of the social supports for the family to which I alluded . . . the position of women and mothers has become more and more isolated. With the breakdown of the community, the neighborhood, and the extended family, an increasing responsibility for the care and upbringing of children has fallen on the young mother. Under these circumstances, it is not surprising that many young women in America are in revolt. I understand and share their sense of rage, but I fear the consequences of some of the solutions they advocate, which will have the effect of isolating children still further from the kind of care and attention they need.[7]

Children *cannot* raise themselves properly. This fact was illustrated again in a recent conversation with a research psychologist who visited my office. He had been studying the early childhoods of inmates at a state prison in Arizona. He and his associates were seeking to discover the common characteristics which the prisoners shared, hoping to unlock the causes for their antisocial behavior. It was initially assumed that poverty would be the common thread, but their findings contradicted these expectations. The inmates came from all socioeconomic levels of society, though most of them attempted to excuse their crimes by professing to have been poor. Instead, the researchers discovered one fundamental characteristic shared by the men:

an absence of adult contact in their early home lives. As children, they spent most of their time in the company of their peers . . . or altogether alone. Such was the childhood of Lee Harvey Oswald, Charles Manson, and many other perpetrators of violent crimes later in life. The conclusion is inescapable: there is no substitute for loving parental leadership in the early development of children.

But my intense personal opinions on this matter of "preschool mothering" are not only based on scientific evidence and professional experience. My views have also been greatly influenced within my own home. Let me share a statement I wrote several years ago in my book *What Wives Wish Their Husbands Knew About Women.*

Our two children are infinitely complex, as are all children, and my wife and I want to guide the formative years ourselves. Danae is nine years old. She will be an adolescent in four more seasons, and I am admittedly jealous of anything robbing me of these remaining days of her childhood. Every moment is precious to me. Ryan is now four. Not only is he in constant motion, but he is also in a state of rapid physical and emotional change. At times it is almost frightening to see how dynamic is the development of my little toddler. When I leave home for a four- or five-day speaking trip, Ryan is a noticeably different child upon my return. The building blocks for his future emotional and physical stability are clearly being laid moment by moment, stone upon stone, precept upon precept. Now I ask you who disagree with what I have written, to whom am I going to submit the task of guiding that unfolding process of development? Who will care enough to make the necessary investment if my wife and I are too busy for the job? What baby-sitter will take our place? What group-oriented facility can possibly provide the individual love and guidance which Ryan and Danae need and deserve? Who will represent my value and beliefs to my son and daughter and be ready to answer their questions during the peak of interest? To whom will I surrender the prime-time experiences of their day? The rest of the world can make its own choice, but as for me and my house, we welcome the opportunity to shape the two little lives which have been loaned to us. And I worry about a nation which calls that task "unrewarding and unfulfilling and boring."

This brings us to the third and final myth to be considered.

3. *Most* mothers of small children can work all day and still have the energy to meet their family obligation . . . perhaps even better than if they remained at home.

There is only so much energy within the human body for expenditure during each twenty-four hours, and when it is invested in one place it is not available for use in another. It is highly improbable that the average woman can arise early in the morning and get her family fed and located for the day, then work from 9:00 to 5:00, drive home from 5:01 to 5:30, and still have the energy to assault her "homework" from 5:31 until midnight. Oh, she may cook dinner and handle major household chores, but few women alive are equipped with the super-strength necessary at the end of a workday to meet the emotional needs of their children, to train and guide and discipline, to build self-esteem, to teach the true values of life, and beyond all that, to maintain a healthy marital relationship as well. Perhaps the task can be accomplished for a week or a month, or even a season. But for years on end? I simply don't believe it. To the contrary, I have observed that exhausted wives and mothers often become irritable, grouchy, and frustrated, setting the stage for conflict within the home. As such, I believe more divorces are caused by mutual overcommitment by husbands and wives than all other factors combined. It is the number one marriage killer!

In summary, circumstances may require that wives and mothers seek full-time employment outside the home. In those instances, Christian onlookers should express tolerant understanding of the person's unspoken needs and obligations. However, the decision for Mom to work has profound implications for her family and especially for her small children. That decision must be made in the full light of reality . . . being unedited by the biases of current social fads. And most importantly, we dare not strip the dignity from the most noble occupation in the universe . . . that of molding little lives during their period of greatest vulnerability.

Let me conclude by sharing a note written to me recently by a ten-year-old boy. He said: "Dear Dr. Dobson, I have a working mom and a working dad and I would like to know what us kids can do. Brian."

I will permit America's parents to respond to Brian's question. They are, after all, the only ones who *can* provide a satisfactory answer to it.[8]

Dear Dr. Dobson:

Enclosed is an article that appeared recently in the *Washington Post* newspaper, which I know you will find interesting. The writer, Mary Fay Bourgoin, is a mother who is employed full time, and expresses her opinions from a secular point of view. Years ago, the Lord taught me the same things she is now learning the hard way. Hope you enjoy the article.

A radio listener

WORKING MOTHERS—SUPERMOMS OR DRONES?

These days it seems that my home, Washington, D.C., is a city of weary women, or, more accurately, exhausted working mothers. For several months, I have been among those who rise at dawn to shower, blow dry their hair, pack lunches, do a load of wash, plug in the crock pot, and glance at the morning paper to make sure the world is not ending before 9 A.M.

Provided there is no last-minute scramble for missing shoes, homework, or show-and-tell items, my three daughters are at school by 8:40 and I am on my way to "the real world."

My job is interesting, working on Capitol Hill as a journalist, investigating the legislative process, interviewing members of Congress—all described in my alumnae magazine as "glamorous." But most of the time I feel that I have one foot on a banana peel and the other on ice.

Balancing marriage, motherhood, and career has become the classic women's problem of the '80s. For those who can pull it all together, life is a first-class act. But judging from my own experience and from talking with other women, life is often a constant round of heartburn, ulcers, and anxiety attacks.

In the '50s, my generation had a different set of pressures. Eighteen years ago I was a college senior. Romanticizing marriage and family life, we talked about weddings, not resumes. Shortly after graduation, the rush began. One by one my classmates, star-struck lovers in wedding satin, stood at flower-decked altars and uttered vows—promises of eternal bliss. We were the color-coordinated generation, never thinking beyond silver patterns, Bermuda honeymoons, and four-bedroom colonials.

In 1964, my views shifted when I experienced my first feminist stirrings on a Greyhound bus from Philadelphia to Washington, D.C. I became engrossed in Betty Friedan's book, *The Feminine Mystique.* It was a page turner. The happy housewife heroine was a myth. Millions of college-educated women, despite career opportunities in a modern society, had been "brainwashed" to believe that their only purpose in life was to find a husband and bear children. Countless women, unable to live up to the feminine ideal, suffered depression, popping bon-bons, booze, or pills to ease their troubled psyches.

As the bus neared Washington, it passed suburban develop-ments, clusters of ranch and split-level houses on treeless lots. I believed that behind all that aluminum siding dwelled misera-ble women wearing chenille bathrobes and muttering, "Is this all?"

Times have changed and so have I. Now I ride the subway into the city. Surrounded by grim-faced women wearing somber dress-for-success suits, aware of my growing uneasiness about some aspects of the feminist movement, I mumble, "Is this lib-eration?"

During the past decade, more and more women entered the labor force—a million a year. According to studies, the number of working mothers has grown more than tenfold since the end of World War II. Although much discussion about career oppor-tunities for women focuses on personal growth and fulfillment, the fact is that the majority of women work because they need the money.

Yet it seems that my generation has now romanticized careers as the cure-all for identity crisis, the supermom syndrome, the housewife blues, and the empty-nest heartache.

Replacing the happy housewife heroine is the successful busi-ness woman who climbs up the corporate ladder without chipping her nail polish, who breezes through the day wearing immaculately tailored clothes, and who returns home, hairdo intact, to an adoring husband and two well-adjusted children.

The sad and obvious truth is that a great many women are now finding out what men have always known—dead-end jobs abound, most work eventually becomes boring, bosses, col-leagues, and clients can be demanding, irritating, and nasty, and it is just as easy to feel trapped and unhappy sitting in a posh office amid the trappings of success as it is standing in the kitchen surrounded by whining preschoolers.

Career-oriented mothers confront still another reality—chil-dren. In some circles it is not fashionable to discuss the dark side of the women's movement and its impact on family life. After all, the experts assure us that it's only a myth that chil-dren of working mothers tend to be sullen, lonely, and neglected. And I, like many, adopted as gospel the feminist pronouncements that if women were free to pursue their professional interests we would be more independent and interesting, more loving wives and mothers.

But the breezy you-can-do-it-all articles leave out an important factor—energy. "Motherhood," as someone recently observed, "saps the energy." And so does a high-pressure career where upward job mobility is a way of life.

Marriage is also demanding, requiring inner strength and motivation to keep a relationship from growing stale. Simply put, when it comes to energy, physical or emotional, we have only so much.

So just as Friedan was tired of reading about the happy, energetic housewife, so I am weary of magazine articles about the successful, dynamic, mother-wife-career wonder woman. In both case histories, something is missing, the unglamorous parts are air-brushed out, the stories bear no relation to reality.

The tales I hear from women—conversations on the subway, concerns exchanged over coffee, instructions whispered over the phone to children, husbands, baby-sitters, teachers— describe the edited-out scenes: sick children sent to school or left home alone, baby-sitters who permit their charges to watch endless hours of television, no-show housekeepers, sleeping babies who are awakened at 6 A.M. and delivered to day care centers at 7 A.M., the growing number of latchkey children—eight- and nine-year-olds who are left on their own after school, unsupervised until a parent returns home—the endless makeshift arrangements for the dreaded school holidays, vacations, snow closings, and other realities that aren't cosmetically attractive for the women's movement.

I suspect these are some of the reasons why feminism has not attracted the poor, the struggling, the blue-collar woman like my mother, who was a seamstress in a shirt factory. For they know all too well the dark underside of the world of working mothers.

"Work," my mother often says, watching from the sidelines as I try successive variations of my marriage-children-career juggling act, "is terribly overrated."

One recent evening on my way home from work, bone-tired, worried about my equally busy husband, a melancholy daughter, and a cantankerous editor, I came across a newspaper article about several celebrity feminists. I read their musings with interest.

"It's nifty," said one, "that women are no longer bound by tra-

ditional role models and careers, that they are now swamped by
options and that they are continuing to challenge sexual stereo-
typing." Yes, I agreed. Yet I had the feeling that she and the
others were naively enthusiastic about the "new woman," view-
ing the world through the wrong end of the binoculars.

When I read how one panelist manages to do it all, my doubts
turned to convictions. Describing the "joys of egalitarianism,"
she said, "My husband and I both work at home. We have a year-
old child whose care is shared equally between the two of us and
a nurse."

I was too tired to laugh.

SECTION 4

DR. DOBSON TALKS ABOUT FAMILIES

Reprinted in the following section is an interview with James Dobson conducted by the editors of *Christian Herald* magazine, and originally published in its July-August, 1979 issue. (Used by permission.)

A CONVERSATION WITH DR. JAMES DOBSON, ONE OF AMERICA'S FOREMOST FAMILY EXPERTS

Dr. Dobson, is there a comprehensive Christian formula for solving family problems?
Albert Einstein spent the last thirty years of his life in a gallant attempt to formulate a unifying theory that would explain all dimensions of physics, but he never succeeded. Likewise, I doubt if the human personality will ever be reduced to a single understanding. We are far too complex to be simplified in that way. From another perspective, however, there is one "formula" that applies to all human relationships, and of course I'm referring to the four-letter word called *love*. Conflicts seem to dissolve themselves when people live according to 1 Corinthians 13 (avoiding boastfulness, irritability, envy, jealousy, selfishness, impatience, rudeness, etc.). The ultimate prescription for harmonious living is contained in that one chapter, and I doubt if any new "discovery" will ever improve on it.

Practically speaking, what does that mean? For example, how does that formula apply to kids who constantly fight and argue?
I'm convinced that many of the emotional problems suffered by some adults can be traced to the viciousness and brutality of siblings and peers during their early home experiences. Self-esteem is a fragile flower, and can easily be crushed by ridicule and mockery occurring routinely between children. But

it need not be so. One of the primary responsibilities of parents
and teachers (especially those within the Christian faith) is to
teach children to love one another. It can be done. Most boys and
girls have a tender spirit beneath the unsympathetic exterior.
Adults who take the time to cultivate that sensitivity can create
a genuine empathy for the handicapped child, the overweight
child, the unattractive child, the retarded child, or the younger
child. But in the absence of that early instruction, a hostile
competitiveness often emerges which can become a barrier to
serving Christ later in life.

**In other words, you see this empathy as an important
element in early Christian training?**
Yes, Jesus gave the highest priority to the expression of love for
God and for our neighbor, yet we often miss this emphasis in
Christian education. For example, many Sunday schools
diligently teach about Moses and Daniel and Joseph, but permit
a chaotic situation to exist, where their cavorting students are
busily mutilating one another's egos. In the absence of strong,
adult leadership at this point, Sunday school can become the
most "dangerous" place in the child's week. I would like to see
teachers spring to the defense of a harassed underdog, and in so
doing, speak volumes about human worth and the love of Jesus.

**There are those who fear you are too authoritarian. They
feel that following your principles too closely will create
too much dogmatism, and that the world already has too
many people who are, in effect, mini-dictators. How do
you answer that criticism?**
Naturally, I don't believe that criticism is justified. I have gone to
great lengths in all my books to warn parents of the dangers of
being harsh and oppressive with their children. One of those
books, *Hide or Seek*, is dedicated in its entirety to the fragile
nature of a child's spirit. Nowhere in my writings will you find a
recommendation that mothers and fathers disregard the
feelings of their boys and girls, or that they use excessive
punishment for childish behavior. What I said is that I believe in
parental leadership—that children should be taught to respect
the benevolent authority of their parents and teachers. If that
makes me authoritarian, then so be it. All I can say in response
is that my own children live in an atmosphere of freedom which

is made possible by *mutual* respect between generations. That two-sided coin is clearly supported in the Scripture which instructs children to obey their parents and then warns parents not to provoke their children to wrath. I like that combination.

How much of a problem is physical chemistry in the feeling cycles we go through? Do they sometimes affect our moral judgments? How do we reconcile these factors with God's demands on our lives? Or put it this way: Isn't it easier to behave better some days than others?
Aren't you asking, "How can God hold us accountable for obedience and compliance when some individuals are apparently not in control of their actions?" Quite honestly, that question has troubled me until recently. The hyperactive child, for example, is often more rebellious and willful than the boy or girl who is calm and serene. How will his defiant nature affect his future relationship with God? What about the sexual deviate who was warped by emotional turmoil during the formative years? What exceptions does God make for the person whose parents specifically taught him immoral and atheistic concepts at home? How about the woman who abuses her child during the stresses of premenstrual tension? What about the person you've described who is possibly driven by chemical forces we don't even comprehend medically?

These issues defy human interpretation, although they no longer distress me from a theological point of view. I have concluded that an infinite God who rules the vast universe is capable of judging those exceptional individuals in a way that will be infinitely just. It is not my business to decipher God's system of evaluation, any more than I can comprehend other aspects of His divine nature. His ways are higher than my ways, and His thoughts are higher than my thoughts. Isn't that why the Bible commands us not to judge one another? We are obviously not equipped to handle the assignment. All I know is that the Lord has required trust and obedience from *me*; as to the reactions of my fellow man I hear Him saying, "What is that to thee? Follow thou Me!"

Do you lend any credence to bio-rhythm theories?
We are biochemical beings, and our bodies definitely operate according to regular patterns and rhythms. A woman's

reproductive system functions on a twenty-eight-day cycle, for example, and there appear to be less obvious patterns in men. Men *and* women also experience "circadian" rhythms or twenty-four-hour oscillations that account for the stresses of "jet lag" among travelers who interfere with their internal clocks. Unfortunately, this chemical understanding has motivated yet another phony theory about the human body and its "fate." Several books on bio-rhythms have led to the notion that the date of one's birth can be used to calculate good days and bad days during adult years. There is not a scrap of evidence to support such a claim.

You don't quote much from the Bible in your counseling materials. Is there a reason why you don't cite the Scriptures more frequently?
Most of my books and tapes were prepared while I have been on the staff of Children's Hospital of Los Angeles and the University of Southern California School of Medicine. This required me to obtain approval from a critical publications committee which reviews everything written by the professional staff. In order to obtain their sanction, I was obligated to take a very casual approach to the Christian application in my books. I now believe the Lord actually motivated this "soft sell" style, because my writings have found a measure of acceptance among those who would not read a more traditional Christian book. Whether right or wrong, however, I've had little choice in the matter. Let me say for the record that all of my views are consistent with my understanding of the Scriptures, and whether or not references are provided, the Bible is my standard.

It's often said that part of the motivation for the study of psychology is that the person wants to know himself or herself. Do you feel you know yourself pretty well? What are the things you need to keep working on?
I'm still getting acquainted with myself and will probably work on that project until I die. And I endure a generous assortment of flaws and shortcomings that I wish I could correct. For example, there's an adolescent characteristic called "ego needs" which surfaces every now and then. I also have to struggle with self-control and self-discipline like everyone else. Nevertheless, God accepts my imperfections and is helping me deal with the changes He requires.

Relative to your arguments about lack of self-esteem, don't you think the Bible in its teaching on original sin says we are inferior?
Absolutely not! We are made in the image of God Himself. He said each of us is worth more than the possession of the entire world, and because of that significance, Jesus was not embarrassed to refer to His followers as brothers. We are, therefore, members of the family of God, which is exclusive company. I believe the Bible teaches that we are to walk humbly before God, "esteeming others higher than ourselves," without groveling in self-doubt and despair. Nowhere do I find a commandment that I am to hate myself and live in shame and personal disgust. However, unfortunately, I know many Christians who are crushed with feelings of inferiority, and some have been taught this concept of worthlessness by their church.

Do you feel that biblical principles and psychological principles (the latter drawn from experience, empirical data, etc.) can be complementary?
Dr. Gary Collins sees modern psychology based on five suppositions which are humanistic and atheistic in substance. They are empiricism, reductionism, relativism, determinism, and naturalism. If that statement is accurate, and I agree that it is, then a Christian psychologist must reject a certain portion of the training he receives in university programs. I have certainly had to do that. But in its place has come a wealth of information about human nature which originated with the Creator of mankind. The Bible offers us a "manufacturer's manual" which I have found to be absolutely valid in the psychology it presents. But to answer your question more directly, there are many instances where traditional psychological understandings are perfectly consistent with biblical teaching.

On what key points do Christian psychologists differ today?
Therapists differ regarding methods of treatment, as do specialists on parenting techniques. I would like to point out, however, that *every* profession is characterized by similar differences in opinion. The Supreme Court often splits 5 to 4 on the issues it considers. And physicians disagree on almost every concept in medicine, although their patients are typically

unaware of the conflict. It is reasonable, therefore, that psychologists—even Christian psychologists—would draw different conclusions about the complex human mind. Until our knowledge of behavior is more complete, there will continue to be differences of views among behavioral scientists.

Would you encourage young people to think of psychology as a strategic vocation from a Christian perspective?
Psychology offers a unique opportunity for a person to be of service as a disciple of Christ. Remember that people usually seek professional help at a time of stress when they are looking for answers, and when they are open to new solutions and alternatives. They have reached a point of vulnerability when the right advice can be very helpful and the wrong counsel can be devastating. I have found it rewarding in my practice to represent the Christian view of marriage, morality, parenting, and honesty, while respecting the right of the individual to make his own choice. What I'm saying is that Christian psychology is a worthy profession for a young believer to pursue, *provided* his own faith is strong enough to withstand the humanistic concepts to which he will be exposed in graduate school. If he begins to compromise on his fundamental beliefs, he could easily become a liability and a hindrance to the Christian faith.

SECTION 5
MALE AND FEMALE UNIQUENESS

How do men and women differ emotionally?
Female emotions are influenced by three exclusively feminine
reproductive functions: menstruation, lactation, and pregnancy. Furthermore, the hypothalamus, which is located at the
base of the brain and has been called the "seat of the emotions,"
is apparently wired very differently for males than for females.
For example, a severe emotional shock or trauma can be inter-
preted by the hypothalamus, which then sends messages to the
pituitary by way of neurons and hormones. The pituitary often
responds by changing the biochemistry of the woman, perhaps
interrupting the normal menstrual cycle for six months or
longer. Female physiology is a finely tuned instrument, being
more complex and vulnerable than the masculine counterpart.
Why some women find that fact insulting is still a mystery to
me.[1]

**You've mentioned some of the ways the sexes differ physi-
ologically and concomitantly in emotional responses.
Could you now describe some of the more *subtle* ways
males and females are unique?**
Medical science has not begun to identify all the ramifications of
sexual uniqueness. The implications are extremely subtle. For
example, when researchers quietly walked on high school and
college campuses to study behavior of the sexes, they observed
that males and females even transported their books in different
ways. The young men tended to carry them at their sides with
their arms looped over the top. Women and girls, by contrast,
usually cradled their books at their breasts, in much the same

way they would a baby. Who can estimate how many other sex-related influences lie below the level of consciousness?

Admittedly, some of the observed differences between the sexes are culturally produced. I don't know how to sort out those which are exclusively genetic from those which represent learned responses. Frankly, it doesn't seem to matter a great deal. The differences exist, for whatever reason, and the current cultural revolution will not alter most of them significantly. At the risk of being called a sexist, or a propagator of sexual stereotypes, or a male chauvinist pig (or worse), let me delineate a few of the emotional patterns typical of women as compared with men.

The reproductive capacity of women results in a greater appreciation for stability, security, and enduring human relationships. In other words, females are more *future*-oriented because of their procreative physiology and its motivating concern for children.

Related to the first item is a woman's emotional investment in her home, which usually exceeds that of her husband. She typically cares more than he about the minor details of the house, family functioning, and such concerns. To cite a personal example, my wife and I decided to install a new gas barbecue unit in our backyard. When the plumber completed the assignment and departed, Shirley and I both recognized that he had placed the appliance approximately six inches too high. I looked at the device and said, "Hmmm, yes sir, he sure made a mistake. That post is a bit too high. By the way, what are we having for dinner tonight?" Shirley's reaction was dramatically different. She said, "The plumber has that thing sticking up in the air and I don't think I can stand it!" Our contrasting views represented a classic difference of emotional intensity relating to the home.

But the sexes are also different in competitive drive. Anyone who doubts that fact should observe how males and females approach a game of Ping-Pong, Monopoly, dominoes, horseshoes, volleyball, or tennis. Women may use the event as an excuse for fellowship and pleasant conversation. For men, the name of the game is *conquest.* Even if the setting is a friendly social gathering in the host's backyard, the beads of sweat on each man's forehead reveal his passion to win. This aggressive competitiveness has been attributed to cultural influences. I don't believe it. As Dr. Richard Restak said in his book, *The Brain! The Lost Frontier:* "At a birthday party for five-year-olds, it's not usually the girls who pull hair, throw punches, or smear each other with food."

Furthermore, a maternal inclination apparently operates in most women, although its force is stronger in some than others. The desire to procreate is certainly evident in those who are unable to conceive. I receive a steady influx of letters from women who express great frustration from their inability to become mothers. Although culture plays a major role in these longings, I believe they are rooted in female anatomy and physiology.

These items are illustrative and are not intended to represent a scientific delineation of male and female differences. Thus, the examples I've listed merely scratch the surface, and you are invited to add your own observations and make your own interpretations.[2]

You have stated in your books that men and women develop self-esteem in a different way. Would you explain that uniqueness?
Men and women have the same needs for self-worth and belonging, but they typically approach those needs from a different angle . . . especially if the woman is a full-time homemaker. A man derives his sense of worth primarily from the reputation he earns in his job or profession. He draws emotional satisfaction from achieving in business, becoming financially independent, developing a highly respected craft or skill, supervising others, becoming "boss," or by being loved and appreciated by his patients, clients, or fellow businessmen. The man who is successful in these areas does not depend on his wife as his *primary* shield against feelings of inferiority. Of course, she plays an important role as his companion and lover, but she isn't essential to his self-respect day by day.

By contrast, a homemaker approaches her marriage from a totally different perspective. She does not have access to "other" sources of self-esteem commonly available to her husband. She can cook a good dinner, but once it is eaten, her family may not even remember to thank her for it. Her household duties do not bring her respect in the community, and she is not likely to be praised for the quality of her dusting techniques. Therefore, the more isolated she becomes, the more vital her man will be to her sense of fulfillment, confidence, and well-being. Let's reduce it to a useful oversimplification: men derive self-esteem by being respected; women feel worthy when they are *loved.* This may be the most important personality distinction between the sexes.[3]

Is the felt need for sex the same in both males and females?
Men and women differ significantly in their manifestations of sexual desire. Recent research seems to indicate that the intensity of pleasure and excitation at the time of orgasm in women and ejaculation in men is about the same for both sexes, although the pathway to that climax takes a different route. Most men can become excited more quickly than women. They may reach a point of finality before their mates get their minds off the evening meal and what the kids will wear tomorrow morning. It is a wise man who recognizes this feminine inertia, and brings his wife along at her own pace.

This coin has two sides, however. Women should also understand how their husbands' needs differ from their own. When sexual response is blocked in males, they experience an accumulating physiological pressure which demands release. Two seminal vesicles (small sacs containing semen) gradually fill to capacity; as maximum level is reached, hormonal influences sensitize the man to all sexual stimuli. Whereas a particular woman would be of little interest to him when he is satisfied, he may be eroticized just to be in her presence when he is in a state of deprivation. A wife may find it difficult to comprehend this accumulating aspect of her husband's sexual appetite, since her needs are typically less urgent and pressing. Thus, she should recognize that his desire is dictated by definite biochemical forces within his body, and if she loves him, she will seek to satisfy those needs as meaningfully and as regularly as possible. I'm not denying that women have definite sexual needs which seek gratification; rather, I am merely explaining that abstinence is usually more difficult for men to tolerate.[4]

Can you be more specific regarding the differences in sexual desire and preferences between males and females? Since I'm getting married next July, I would like to know how my future husband's need will differ from my own. Could you summarize the major distinctions that will occur between us?
You are wise to ask this question, because the failures to understand male and female preferences often produces a continual source of marital frustration and guilt.

First, men are primarily aroused by *visual* stimulation. They are turned on by feminine nudity or peek-a-boo glimpses of semi-nudity. Women, on the other hand, are much less visually

oriented than men. Sure,they are interested in attractive masculine bodies, but the physiological mechanism of sex is not
triggered, typically, by what they see; women are stimulated primarily by the sense of touch. Thus, we encounter the first
source of disagreement in the bedroom; he wants her to appear
unclothed in a lighted room, and she wants him to caress her in
the dark.

Second, and much more important, men are not very discriminating in regard to the person living within an interesting body.
A man can walk down a street and be stimulated by a scantily
clad female who shimmies past him, even though he knows
nothing about her personality or values or mental capabilities.
He is attracted by her body itself. Likewise, he can become
almost as excited over a photograph of an unknown nude model
as he can in a face-to-face encounter with someone he loves. In
essence, the sheer biological power of sexual desire in a male is
largely focused on the physical body of an attractive female.
Hence, there is some validity to the complaint by women that
they have been used as "sex objects" by men. This explains
why female prostitutes outnumber males by a wide margin and
why few women try to "rape" men. It explains why a roomful of
toothless old men can get a large charge from watching a bur-
lesque dancer "take it all off." It reflects the fact that masculine
self-esteem is more motivated by a desire to "conquer" a woman
than in becoming the object of her romantic love. These are not
very flattering characteristics of male sexuality, but they are
well documented in the professional literature.

Women, on the other hand, are much more discriminating in
their sexual interests. They less commonly become excited by
observing a good-looking charmer, or by the photograph of a
hairy model; rather, their desire is usually focused on a particular individual whom they respect or admire. A woman is
stimulated by the romantic aura which surrounds her man, and
by his character and personality. She yields to the man who
appeals to her emotionally as well as physically. Obviously,
there are exceptions to these characteristic desires, but the fact
remains: sex for men is a more physical phenomenon; sex for
women is a deeply emotional experience.[5]

**You've discussed physical differences between the sexes
as related to reproduction. Could you list the other *physical* characteristics of males and females?**
Dr. Paul Popenoe, the late founder of the American Institute of

Family Relations in Los Angeles, wrote a brief article on the subject you have raised. I will let him respond to the question, *Are Women Really Different?*[6]

1. Men and women differ in every cell of their bodies. This difference in the chromosome combination is the basic cause of development into maleness or femaleness as the case may be.

2. Woman has greater constitutional vitality, perhaps because of this chromosome difference. Normally, she outlives man by three or four years in the U.S.

3. The sexes differ in their basal metabolism—that of woman being normally lower than that of man.

4. They differ in skeletal structure, woman having a shorter head, broader face, chin less protruding, shorter legs, and longer trunk. The first finger of a woman's hand is usually longer than the third; with men the reverse is true. Boys' teeth last longer than do those of girls.

5. Woman has a larger stomach, kidneys, liver, and appendix, and smaller lungs.

6. In function, woman has several very important ones totally lacking in man—menstruation, pregnancy, lactation. All of these influence behavior and feelings. She has more different hormones than does man. The same gland behaves differently in the two sexes—thus woman's thyroid is larger and more active; it enlarges during pregnancy but also during menstruation; it makes her more prone to goiter, provides resistance to cold, is associated with the smooth skin, relatively hairless body, and thin layer of subcutaneous fat which are important elements in the concept of personal beauty. It also contributes to emotional instability—she laughs and cries more easily.

7. Woman's blood contains more water (20 percent fewer red cells). Since these supply oxygen to the body cells, she tires more easily, is more prone to faint. Her constitutional viability is therefore strictly a long-range matter. When the working day in British factories, under wartime conditions, was increased from ten to twelve hours, accidents of women increased 150 percent, of men not at all.

8. In brute strength, men are 50 percent above women.

9. Woman's heart beats more rapidly (80, versus 72 for men); blood pressure (ten points lower than man) varies from minute to minute; but she has much less tendency to

high blood pressure—at least until after the menopause.

10. Her vital capacity or breathing power is lower in the 7:10 ratio.

11. She stands high temperature better than does man; metabolism slows down less.[7]

SECTION 6

THE MEANING OF MASCULINITY

It is apparent from reading your book, *Straight Talk to Men and Their Wives,* that you are a strong advocate of masculine leadership at home. What response do you offer to activist women who would consider this view to be chauvinistic and archaic?

It is important to understand what I mean by masculine leadership. I don't attempt to justify men who oppress their children or show disregard for the needs and wishes of their wives. That kind of nineteenth century authoritarianism is dead, and may it rest in peace. However, I do believe that the Scriptures (which are the standard by which I measure *everything*) make it clear that men have been assigned the primary responsibility for the provision of authority in the home. At least, this is the way I understand the biblical prescription. Ephesians 5:22-28 states:

> Wives, be subject to your husbands, as to the Lord. For the husband is the head of the wife as Christ is the head of the church, his body, and is himself its Savior. As the church is subject to Christ, so let wives also be subject in everything to their husbands. Husbands, love your wives, as Christ loved the church and gave himself up for her, that he might sanctify her, having cleansed her by the washing of water with the word, that he might present the church to himself in splendor, without spot or wrinkle or any such thing, that she might be holy and without blemish. Even so husbands should love their wives as their own bodies. He who loves his wife loves himself (RSV).

This Scripture, combined with the many others relating to wives' submission to husbands' authority (1 Peter 3:1 KJV, for example: "Likewise, ye wives, be in subjection to your own husbands; that, if any obey not the word, they also may without the word be won by the conversation of the wives.") makes it clear to me that a Christian man is obligated to lead his family to the best of his ability. God apparently expects a man to be the ultimate decision-maker in his family. Likewise, he bears heavier responsibility for the outcome of those decisions. If his family has purchased too many items on credit, then the financial crunch is ultimately his fault. If the family never reads the Bible or seldom goes to church on Sunday, God holds the man to blame. If the children are disrespectful and disobedient, the primary responsibility lies with the father . . . not his wife. (I don't remember Eli's wife being criticized for raising two evil sons; it was her husband who came under God's wrath. See 1 Samuel 3:13.)

From this perspective, what happens to a family when the designated leader doesn't do his job? Similar consequences can be seen in a corporation whose president only pretends to direct the company. The organization disintegrates very quickly. The parallel to leaderless families is too striking to be missed. In my view, America's greatest need is for husbands to begin guiding their families, rather than pouring every physical and emotional resource into the mere acquisition of money.[1]

Would you be more specific about the relationship between the sexes? Am I to assume you do not favor a fifty-fifty arrangement in the husband-wife interaction?
That is correct. However, let me offer two opinions about the ideal relationship between husbands and wives that may clarify my viewpoint. First, because of the fragile nature of the male ego and a man's enormous need to be respected, combined with female vulnerability and a woman's need to be loved, I feel it is a mistake to tamper with the time-honored relationship of husband as loving protector and wife as recipient of that protection.

Second, because two captains sink the ship and two cooks spoil the broth, I feel that a family must have a leader whose decisions prevail in times of differing opinions. If I understand the Scriptures, that role has been assigned to the man of the house. However, he must not incite his crew to mutiny by heavy-handed disregard for their feelings and needs. He should, in fact, put the best interests of his family above his own, even to the point of death, if necessary. Nowhere in Scripture is he authorized to become a dictator or slave-owner.

Other combinations of husband-wife teamwork have been successful in individual families, but I've seen many complications occurring in marriages where the man was passive, weak, and lacking in qualities of leadership. None of the modern alternatives has improved on the traditional masculine role as prescribed in the Good Book. It was, after all, inspired by the Creator of mankind.[2]

Much has been written and said recently about the "macho" man who is unable to reveal his true emotions and feelings. Do you agree that American men have too tight a rein on their emotions and should learn to loosen them up?

Perhaps so. It is important for men to be willing (and able) to cry and love and hope. My father, who symbolized masculinity for me, was a very tender man who was not ashamed to weep. On the other hand, there are dangers in permitting emotions to rule our minds. Feelings must not dominate rational judgment, especially in times of crisis, nor should we allow the minor frustrations of living to produce depression and despair. Both men and women must learn to ventilate their feelings and be "real" people, without yielding to the tyranny of fluctuating emotions.[3]

What do you feel is a father's number one priority?

His most important responsibility, I believe, is to communicate the real meaning of Christianity to his children. This mission can be likened to a three-man relay race. First, your father runs his lap around the track, carrying the baton, which represents the gospel of Jesus Christ. At the appropriate moment, he hands the baton to you, and you begin your journey around the track. Then finally, the time will come when you must get the baton safely in the hands of your children. But as any track coach will testify, *relay races are won or lost in the transfer of the baton.* There is a critical moment when all can be lost by a fumble or miscalculation. The baton is rarely dropped on the back side of the track when the runner has it firmly in his grasp. If failure is to occur, it will probably happen in the exchange between generations.

According to the Christian values which govern my life, my most important reason for living is to get the baton, the gospel, safely in the hands of my children. Of course, I want to place it in as many other hands as possible; *nevertheless, my number one responsibility is to evangelize my own children.* I hope millions of other fathers agree with that ultimate priority.[4]

I agree with your belief that the father should be the spiritual leader in the family, but it just doesn't happen that way at our house. If the kids go to church on Sunday, it's because I wake them up and see that they get ready. If we have family devotions, it's done at my insistence, and I'm the one who prays with the children at bedtime. If I didn't do these things, our kids would have no spiritual training. Nevertheless, people keep saying that I should wait for my husband to accept spiritual leadership in our family. What do you advise in my situation?

That's an extremely important question, and a subject of some controversy right now. As you indicated, some Christian leaders instruct women to wait passively for their husbands to assume spiritual responsibility. Until that leadership is accepted, they recommend that wives stay out of the way and let God put pressure on the husband to assume the role that He's given to men. I strongly disagree with that view when small children are involved. If the issue focused only on the spiritual welfare of a husband and wife, then a woman could afford to bide her time. However, the presence of boys and girls changes the picture dramatically. Every day that goes by without spiritual training for them is a day that can never be recaptured.

Therefore, if your husband is not going to accept the role of spiritual leadership that God has given him, then I believe you must do it. You have no time to lose. You should continue taking the family to church on Sunday. You should pray with the children and teach them to read the Bible. Furthermore, you must continue your private devotions and maintain your own relationship with God. In short, I feel that the spiritual life of children (and adults) is simply too important for a woman to postpone for two or four or six years, hoping her husband will eventually awaken. Jesus made it clear that members of our own family can erect the greatest barriers to our faith, but must not be permitted to do so. He says, "Do not think that I have come to bring peace on earth; I have not come to bring peace, but a sword. For I have come to set a man against his father, and a daughter against her mother, and a daughter-in-law against her mother-in-law; and a man's foes will be those of his own household. He who loves father or mother more than me is not worthy of me; and he who loves son or daughter more than me is not worthy of me" (Matt. 10:34-37 RSV).

This conflict has been experienced with our own family. My grandfather, R. L. Dobson, was a moral man who saw no need for the Christian faith. His spiritual disinterest placed my grandmother, Juanita Dobson, under great pressure, for she was a devout Christian who felt she must put God first. Therefore, she accepted the responsibility of introducing her six children to Jesus Christ. There were times when my grandfather exerted tremendous pressure on her, not to give up the faith, but to leave him out of it.

He said, "I am a good father and provider, I pay my bills, and I am honest in dealing with my fellow man. That is enough."

His wife replied, "You are a good man, but that is *not* enough. You should give your heart to God." This he could not comprehend.

My 97-pound grandmother made no attempt to force her faith on her husband, nor did she treat him disrespectfully. But she quietly continued to pray and fast for the man she loved. For more than forty years she brought this same petition before God on her knees.

Then at sixty-nine years of age, my grandfather suffered a stroke, and for the first time in his life he was desperately ill. One day his young daughter came into his room to clean and straighten. As she walked by his bed, she saw tears in his eyes. No one had ever seen him cry before.

"Daddy, what's wrong?" she asked.

He responded, "Honey, go to the head of the stairs and call your mother."

My grandmother ran to her husband's side and heard him say, "I know I'm going to die and I'm not afraid of death, but it's so dark. There's no way out. I've lived my whole life through and missed the one thing that really matters. Will you pray for me?"

"Will I pray?" exclaimed my grandmother. She had been hoping for that request throughout her adult life. She fell to her knees and the intercessions of forty years seemed to pour out through that bedside prayer. R. L. Dobson gave his heart to God that day in a wonderful way.

During the next two weeks, he asked to see some of the

church people whom he had offended and requested their forgiveness. He concluded his personal affairs and then died with a testimony on his lips. Before descending into a coma from which he would never awaken, my grandfather said, ". . . Now there is a way through the darkness."

The unrelenting prayers of my little grandmother had been answered.

Returning to the question, I would like to caution women not to become "self-righteous" and critical of their husbands. Let everything be done in a spirit of love. However, there may be some lonely years when the burden of spiritual leadership with children must be carried alone. If that is the case, the Lord has promised to walk with you through these difficult days.[5]

I keep hearing that it is unwise to get too carried away with the successes of your kids, but I can't help it. Is it wrong for me to feel a sense of fatherly pride when my son succeeds in basketball? How can I not *care* about the quality of his performance?

There's nothing wrong about feeling good about the successes of our children. The problem occurs when parents care *too much* about those triumphs and failures . . . when their own egos are riding on the kids' performances . . . when winning is necessary to maintain their parents' respect and love. Boys and girls should know they are accepted simply because they are God's own creation. That is enough!

I'm reminded of John McKay, the former football coach from the University of Southern California. I saw him interviewed on television at a time when his son, John, Junior, was a successful football player on the USC team. The interviewer referred to John's athletic talent and asked Coach McKay to comment on the pride he must feel over his son's accomplishments on the field. His answer was most impressive:

"Yes, I'm pleased that John had a good season last year. He does a fine job and I am proud of him. But I would be just as proud if he had never played the game at all."

Coach McKay was saying, in effect, that John's football talent is recognized and appreciated, but his human worth does not depend on his ability to play football. Thus, his son would not lose respect if the next season brought failure and disappointment. John's place in his dad's heart was secure, being independent of his performance. I wish every child could say the same.

Traditionally, fathers have been relatively uninvolved in the discipline of preschool children. How do you feel about the importance of paternal involvement?
It is extremely important for fathers to help discipline and participate in the parenting process when possible. Children need their fathers and respond to their masculine manner, of course, but wives need the involvement of their husbands, too. This is especially true of homemakers who have done combat duty through the long day and find themselves in a state of battle fatigue by nightfall. Husbands get tired too, of course, but if they can hold together long enough to help get the little tigers in bed, nothing could contribute more to the stability of their homes. I am especially sympathetic with the mother who is raising a toddler or two and an infant at the same time. There is no more difficult assignment on the face of the earth. Husbands who recognize this fact can help their wives feel understood, loved, and supported in the vital jobs they are doing.[6]

Our two children will obey my husband with just a word from him, even responding to a slight frown when we are in a group setting. But I have to scream and threaten to make them mind. Why do you suppose this is true?
That difference in response usually results from the factors: (1) The father is more likely to back up his commands with *action* if the children don't obey, and the kids know it; (2) The mother spends more time with the children, and as they say, "familiarity breeds contempt"—her authority gradually erodes under constant pressure.

There is another phenomenon at work, however, which I would like to consider in greater detail. I'm referring to the fact that children naturally look to their father for authority. When our son Ryan was four years old, he overheard a reference to my childhood.

"Daddy, were you ever a little boy?" he asked.

"Yes, Ryan, I was smaller than you," I replied.

"Were you ever a baby?" he inquired with disbelief.

"Yes. Everyone is a tiny baby when he is born."

Ryan looked puzzled. He simply could not comprehend his 6-foot 2-inch, 190-pound father as an infant. He thought for a minute and then said, "Were you a daddy-baby?"

It was impossible for Ryan to imagine me without the mantle of authority, even if I were a tiny newborn. His nine-year-old sister reacted similarly the first time she was shown home movies of me when I was only four. There on the screen was a baby-faced, innocent lad on a horse. Danae had to be assured that the picture was of me, whereupon she exclaimed, "That kid spanks me?"

Danae and Ryan both revealed their perception of me . . . not as a man who had been given authority . . . but as a man who *was* authority. Such is the nature of childhood. Boys and girls typically look to their fathers, whose size and power and deeper voices bespeak leadership. That's why, despite numerous exceptions, men teachers are likely to handle classroom discipline more easily that soft ladies with feminine voices. (A woman teacher once told me that the struggle to control her class was like trying to keep thirty-two Ping-Pong balls under water at the same time.)

That is also why mothers need the disciplinary involvement of their husbands. Not that a man must handle every act of disobedience, but he should serve as the frame on which parental authority is constructed. Furthermore, it must be clear to the kids that Dad is in agreement with Mother's policies and he will defend her in instances of insurrection. Referring to 1 Timothy 3:4, this is what is meant by a father having the "proper authority in his own household."[7]

What is the "mid-life" crisis that many men experience?

It is a time of intense personal evaluation when frightening and disturbing thoughts surge through a man's mind, posing questions about who he is and why he's here and what it all matters. It is a period of self-doubt and disenchantment with everything familiar and stable. It represents terrifying thoughts that can't be admitted or revealed even to those closest to him. These anxieties often produce an uncomfortable separation between loved ones at a time when support and understanding are desperately needed.[8]

When does the mid-life crisis typically occur and how universal is it among men?

This time of self-doubt usually occurs during the third or fourth decades of life, but can transpire during the fifth. Concerning the incidence, Lee Stockford reported the findings of three studies involving more than 2100 persons and concluded that 80 percent of the executives between thirty-four and forty-two years of age experience a mid-life trauma of some variety. This estimate is consistent with my own observations, especially among highly motivated, successful business and professional men.[9]

What does a man experience during a full-fledged mid-life crisis?

Dr. Jim Conway has written a book called *Men in Mid-Life Crisis* (David C. Cook, 1978) which I recommend highly. In it, he identifies four major "enemies" which plague a man entering this stressful period. The first is his own body. There is no doubt about it; that guy they called "Joe College" just a few years ago is now growing older. His hair is falling out, despite desperate attempts to coddle and protect every remaining strand. "Me, bald?" he shudders. Then he notices he doesn't have the stamina he once had. He begins getting winded on escalators. Before long, words assume new meanings for Ol' Joe. "The rolling stones" are in his gall bladder and "speed" (which once referred to amphetamines or fast driving) is his word for prune juice. He takes a business trip and the stewardess offers him "coffee, tea, or milk of magnesia." The cells in his face then pack up and run south for the winter, leaving a shocked and depressed Joseph standing two inches from the mirror in disbelief.

To summarize this first great concern of the mid-life years, a man approaching forty is forced to admit: (1) he is getting older; (2) the changes produced by aging are neither attractive nor convenient; (3) in a world that equates human worth with youth and beauty, he is about to suffer a personal devaluation; and (4) old age is less than two decades away, bringing eventual sickness and death. When a man confronts this package for the first time, he is certain to experience an emotional reverberation from its impact.

The second enemy facing a man in his mid-life years is his work. He typically resents his job and feels trapped in the field he has chosen. Many blue- and white-collar workers wish they'd had the opportunity to study medicine or law or dentistry. Little do they realize that physicians and attorneys and orthodontists often wish they had selected less demanding occupations . . . jobs that could be forgotten on evenings and weekends . . . jobs that didn't impose the constant threat of malpractice suits . . . jobs that left time for recreation and hobbies. This occupational unrest at all socioeconomic levels reaches a peak of intensity in the middle years, when the new awareness of life's brevity makes men reluctant to squander a single day that remains. But, on the other hand, they have little choice. The financial needs of their families demand that they keep pressing . . . so the kids can go to college . . . so the house payment can be met . . . so the lives they have known can continue. Thus, their emotions are caught in an ever-tightening vise.

The third enemy that rises to confront a middle-aged man is, believe it or not, his own family. These stormy years of self-doubt and introspection can be devastating to marriage. Such a man often becomes angry and depressed and rebellious toward those closest to him. He resents the fact that his wife and kids need him. No matter how hard he works, they always require more money than he can earn, and that agitates him further. At a time when he is in a selfish mood, wanting to meet his own needs, it seems that every member of the family is pulling on him. Even his parents have now become his financial and emotional responsibility. Again, he is seized by the urge to run.

The fourth and final enemy of a man in mid-life crisis appears to be God Himself. Through a strange manipulation of logic, man blames the Creator for all his troubles, approaching Him with rebellion and anger. In return, he feels condemned and abandoned and unloved by God. The consequence is a weakened faith and a crumbling system of beliefs. This explains, more than any other factor, the radical changes in behavior that often accompany the struggles of middle life.

Let me give this latter point the strongest possible emphasis. One of the most common observations made by relatives and friends of a man in mid-life crisis reflects this sudden reversal of personality and behavior.

"I don't understand what happened to Loren," a wife will say. "He seemed to change overnight from a stable, loving husband and father to an irresponsible rogue. He quit going to church. He began openly flirting with other women. He lost interest in our sons. Even his clothing became more modish and flamboyant. He started combing his hair forward to hide his baldness and he bought a new sports car that we couldn't afford. I just can't figure out what suddenly came over my dependable husband."

This man has obviously experienced the changes we have described, but his *basic* problem is spiritual in nature. As his system of beliefs disintegrated, then his commitment to related biblical concepts was weakened accordingly. Monogamy, fidelity, responsibility, life after death, self-denial, Christian witnessing, basic honesty, and dozens of other components of his former faith suddenly became invalid or suspect. The result was a rapid and catastrophic change in lifestyle which left his family and friends in a state of confusion and shock. This pattern has occurred for thousands of families in recent years.[10]

I am twenty-nine years old and want to avoid a mid-life crisis, if possible. What causes this period of trauma, and how can I head it off?
It is my firm conviction that mid-life crisis results from what the Bible refers to as "building your house upon sand." It is possible to be a follower of Jesus Christ and accept His forgiveness from sin, yet still be deeply influenced by the values and attitudes of one's surrounding culture. Thus, a young Christian husband and father may become a workaholic, a hoarder of money, a status-seeker, a worshiper of youth, and a lover of pleasure. These tendencies may not reflect his conscious choices and desires; they merely represent the stamp of society's godless values on his life and times.

Despite his unchristian attitudes, the man may appear to "have it all together" in his first fifteen years as an adult, especially if he is successful in early business pursuits. But he is in considerable danger. Whenever we build our lives on values and principles that contradict the time-honored wisdom of God's Word, we are laying a foundation on the sand. Sooner or later, the storms will howl and the structure we have laboriously constructed will collapse with a mighty crash.

Stated succinctly, a mid-life crisis is more likely to be severe for those whose values reflect the temporal perspectives of this world. A man does not mourn the loss of his youth, for example, if he honestly believes that his life is merely a preparation for a better one to follow. And God does not become the enemy of a man who has walked and talked with Him in daily communion and love. And the relationship between a man and wife is less strained in the mid-life years if they have protected and maintained their friendship since they were newlyweds. In short, the mid-life crisis represents a day of reckoning for a lifetime of wrong values, unworthy goals, and ungodly attitudes.

Perhaps this explains my observation that most men in the throes of a mid-life crisis are long-term workaholics. They have built their mighty castles on the sandy beach of materialism, depending on money and status and advancement and success to meet all their needs. They reserved no time for wife, children, friends, and God. Drive! Push! Hustle! Scheme! Invest! Prepare! Anticipate! Work! Fourteen-hour days were followed by week-ends at the office and forfeited vacations and midnight oil. Then after twenty years of this distorted existence, they suddenly have cause to question the value of it all. "Is this really what I want to do with my life?" they ask. They realize too late that they have frantically climbed the ladder of success, only to discover that it was leaning against the wrong wall.[11]

You are describing me, virtually word for word. Will I always be this depressed and miserable?
No. A mid-life crisis has a predictable beginning and end. An analogy to adolescence is helpful at this point: both periods are relatively short-term, age-related times of transition which produce intense anxiety, self-doubt, introspection, and agitation. Fortunately, however, neither adolescence nor the mid-life years represent permanent traps which hold victims captive. Rather, they can be thought of as doors through which we must all pass and from which we will all emerge. What I'm saying is that *normality will return* (unless you make some disruptive mistakes in a desperate attempt to cope).[12]

A final comment to the confirmed workaholic: I have examined America's breathless lifestyle and find it to be *unacceptable*. At forty-three years of age (I would be forty-four but I was sick a year), I have been thinking about the stages of my earthly existence and what they will represent at its conclusion. There was a time when all of my friends were graduating from high school. Then I recall so many who entered colleges around the country. And alas, I lived through a phase when everyone seemed to be getting married. Then a few years later, we were besieged by baby shower announcements. You see, my generation is slowly but relentlessly moving through the decades, as have 2400 generations that preceded it. Now, it occurs to me that a time will soon come when my friends will be dying. ("Wasn't it tragic what happened to Charles Painter yesterday?")

My aunt, Naomi Dobson, wrote me shortly before her death in 1978. She said, "It seems like every day another of my close friends either passes away or is afflicted with a terrible disease." Obviously, she was in that final phase of her generation. Now she is also gone.

What does this have to do with my life today? How does it relate to yours? I'm suggesting that we stop and consider the brevity of our years on earth, perhaps finding new motivation to preserve the values that will endure. Why should we work ourselves into an early grave, missing those precious moments with loved ones who crave our affection and attention? It is a question that every man and woman should consider.

Let me offer this final word of encouragement for those who are determined to slow the pace: once you get out from under constant pressure, you'll wonder why you drove yourself so hard for all those years. *There is a better way!*[13]

SECTION 7

ADULT SEXUALITY

Why are some men and women less sensual than others?
Adult attitudes toward sexual relations are largely conditioned
during childhood and adolescence. It is surprising to observe
how many otherwise well-adjusted people still think of married
sex as dirty, animalistic, or evil. Such a person who has been
taught a one-sided, negative approach to sex during the
formative years may find it impossible to release these carefully
constructed inhibitions on the wedding night. The marriage
ceremony is simply insufficient to reorient one's attitude from
"Thou shalt not" to "Thou shalt—regularly and with great
passion!" That mental turnabout is not easily achieved.

But I should emphasize another factor: Not all differences in
intensity of the sex drive can be traced to errors in childhood
instruction. Human beings differ in practically every
characteristic. Our feet come in different sizes; our teeth are
shaped differently; some folks eat more than others, and some
are taller than their peers. We are unequal creatures.
Accordingly, we differ in sexual appetites. Our intellectual
"computers" are clearly programmed differently through the
process of genetic inheritance. Some of us "hunger and thirst"
after our sexuality, while others take it much more casually.
Given this variability, we should learn to accept ourselves
sexually, as well as physically and emotionally. This does not
mean that we shouldn't try to improve the quality of our sex
lives, but it does mean that we should stop struggling to achieve
the impossible—trying to set off an atomic bomb with a
matchstick!

As long as husband and wife are satisfied with each other, it
doesn't matter what *Cosmopolitan* magazine says their

inadequacies happen to be. Sex has become a statistical monster. "The average couple has intercourse three times a week! Oh no! What's wrong with us? Are we undersexed?" A husband worries if his genitalia are of "average" size, while his wife contemplates her insufficient bust line. We are tyrannized by the great, new "sexual freedom" which has beset us. I hereby make a proposal: let's keep sex in its proper place; sure it is important, but it should serve us and not the other way around![1]

My wife has very little sexual desire, despite the fact that we love each other and take a lot of time to be together. She reports that this lack of sex drive is extremely depressing to her, and she is in therapy now to help her deal with it. I want to understand better what she is feeling. Can you help me?
It is certain that she is keenly aware of the erotic explosion which burns throughout her society. While her grandmother could have hidden her private inhibitions behind the protection of verbal taboo, today's unresponsive woman is reminded of her inadequacy almost hourly. Radio, television, books, magazines, and movies make her think that the entire human race plunges into orgies of sexual ecstasy every night of the year. An inhibited wife can easily get the notion that the rest of America lives on Libido Lane in beautiful downtown Passion Park while she resides on the lonely side of Blizzard Boulevard. This unparalleled emphasis on genital gymnastics creates emotional pressure in enormous proportions. How frightening to feel sexless in a day of universal sensuality!

Sexual misfires—those icy bedroom encounters which leave both partners unsatisfied and frustrated—tend to be self-perpetuating. Unless each orgasm is accompanied by roman candles, skyrockets, and "The Stars and Stripes Forever," the fear of failure begins to gnaw on body and soul. Every disappointing experience is likely to interfere with the ability to relax and enjoy the next episode, which puts double stress on all those which follow. It is easy to see how this chain reaction of anxieties can assassinate whatever minimal desire was there in the first place. Then when sex finally loses its appeal, great emotions sweep down on the unresponsive lover. A woman who finds no pleasure in intercourse usually feels like a failure as a wife; she fears she may not be able to "hold" her

husband who faces flirtatious alternatives at the office. She
experiences incredible guilt for her inability to respond, and
inevitably her self-esteem gets clobbered in the process.

With this understanding, it should be obvious what you as her
husband can do to reduce the anxieties and restore her
confidence.[2]

**You said that failure to understand sexual uniqueness can
produce a continual state of marital frustration and guilt.
Will you explain that concern further?**

Even where genuine love is evident, feminine emotions are
critical to sexual response. Unless a woman feels a certain
closeness to her husband at a particular time—unless she
believes he respects her as a person—she may be unable to
enjoy a sexual encounter with him. To the contrary, a man can
come home from work in a bad mood, spend the evening slaving
over his desk or in his garage, watch the eleven o'clock news in
silence, and finally hop into bed for a brief nighttime romp. The
fact that he and his wife have had no tender moments in the
entire evening does not inhibit his sexual desire significantly. He
sees her on her way to bed in her clingy nightgown and that is
enough to throw his switch. But his wife is not so easily moved.
She waited for him all day, and when he came home and hardly
even greeted her, she felt disappointment and rejection. His
continuing coolness and self-preoccupation put a padlock on
her desires: therefore, she may find it impossible to respond to
him later in the evening.

Let me go one step further: when a woman makes love in the
absence of romantic closeness, she feels like a prostitute.
Instead of participating in a mutually exciting interchange
between lovers, she feels used. In a sense, her husband has
exploited her body to gratify himself. Thus, she may either
refuse to submit to his request, or else she will yield with
reluctance and resentment. The inability to explain this
frustration is, I believe, a continual source of agitation to
women.

If I had the power to communicate only one message to every
family in America, I would specify the importance of romantic
love to every aspect of feminine existence. It provides for a
woman's self-esteem, her joy in living, and her sexual
responsiveness. Therefore, the vast number of men who are

involved in bored, tired marriages—and find themselves locked out of the bedroom—should know where the trouble possibly lies. Real love can melt an iceberg.[3]

I find that I am easily distracted during intimate moments, especially by the fear of being overheard by the kids. This doesn't seem to bother my husband at all. Am I being foolish to worry about such things?

Your problem is very common among women, who are typically more easily distracted than men; they are also more aware of the "geography" of sex, the techniques of lovemaking, and the noises and smells than are their husbands. Privacy is often more important to women, too.

Another rather common inhibitor to women, according to the concerns verbalized in counseling sessions, is the lack of cleanliness by their husbands. A service station operator or a construction worker may become sexually aroused by something he has seen or read during the day, causing him to desire intercourse with his wife as soon as he arrives home from his job. He may be sweaty and grimy from the day's work, smelling of body odor and needing to use some Crest on his teeth. Not only are his fingernails dirty, but his rough, calloused hands are irritating to his wife's delicate skin. An interference such as this can paralyze a woman sexually, and make her husband feel rejected and angry.

Spontaneity has its place in the marital bed, but "sudden sex" often results in "sudden failure" for a less passionate woman. In general, I believe sex should be planned for, prepared for, and anticipated. For the man who has been dissatisfied with his recent sex life, I suggest that he call a local hotel or motel and make reservations for a given night, but tell no one about his plans. He might arrange secretly for the children to be cared for until morning, and then ask his wife to go out to dinner with him. After they have eaten a good meal, he should drive to the hotel without going home or announcing his intentions. The element of surprise and excitement should be preserved to the very last moment. Once inside the hotel room (where flowers may be waiting), their hormones will dictate the remainder of the instructions. My point is that sexual excitation requires a little creativity, particularly in cases of a "tired" relationship. For example, the widespread notion that males are inherently active and females are inherently passive in a sexual sense is nonsense; the freedom to express passion spontaneously is vital to enjoyment. When one makes love in the same old bedroom, from the same position and surrounded by the same four walls, it *has* to become rather routine after so many years. And routine sex is usually bored sex.[4]

My husband and I don't get in bed until nearly midnight every evening, and then I'm too tired to really get into love making. Is there something unusual or wrong with me for being unable to respond when the opportunity presents itself?

There is nothing unusual about your situation. Physical exhaustion plays a significant part in many women's inability to respond sexually, and you are one of them. By the time a mother has struggled through an eighteen-hour day—especially if she has been chasing an ambitious toddler or two—her internal pilot light may have flickered and gone out. When she finally falls into bed, sex represents an obligation rather than a pleasure. It is the last item on her "to do" list for that day. Meaningful sexual relations utilize great quantities of body energy and are seriously hampered when those resources have already been expended. Nevertheless, intercourse is usually scheduled as the final event in the evening.

If sex is important in a marriage, and we all know that it is, then some prime time should be reserved for its expression. The day's working activities should end early in the evening, permitting a husband and wife to retire before exhausting themselves on endless chores and responsibilities. Remember this: *whatever* is put at the bottom of your priority list will probably be done inadequately. For too many families, sex languishes in last place.

You may have read Dr. David Reuben's best-selling book entitled, *What You've Always Wanted to Know about Sex but Were Afraid to Ask*. (I bought Dr. Reuben's book because I've always liked his sandwich so well.) But after considering the frequent inhibitions caused by utter exhaustion, I think Dr. Reuben should have called his book, *What You've Always Wanted to Know about Sex but Were Too Tired to Ask!*[5]

My husband and I never talk about the subject of sex, and this is frustrating to me. Is this a common problem in marriage?

It is, especially for those who are having sexual difficulties. It is even more important that the doors of communication be kept open in marriage where sex is a problem. When intercourse has been unenthusiastic, and when anxiety has been steadily accumulating, the tendency is to eliminate all reference to the topic in everyday conversation. Neither partner knows what to do about the problem, and they tacitly agree to ignore it. Even during sexual relations, they do not talk to one another.

One woman wrote me recently to say that her sex life with her husband resembled a "silent movie." Not a word was ever spoken.

How incredible it seems that an inhibited husband and wife can make love several times a week for a period of years without ever verbalizing their feelings or frustrations on this important aspect of their lives. When this happens, the effect is like taking a hot Coke bottle and shaking it until the contents are ready to explode. Remember this psychological law: any anxiety-producing thought or condition which cannot be expressed is almost certain to generate inner pressure and stress. The more unspeakable the subject, the greater the pressurization. And as I have described, anxious silence leads to the destruction of sexual desire.

Furthermore, when conversation is prohibited on the subject of sex, the act of intercourse takes on the atmosphere of a "performance"—each partner feeling that he is being critically evaluated by the other. To remove these communication barriers, the husband should take the lead in helping his wife to verbalize her feelings, her fears, her aspirations. They should talk about the manners and techniques which stimulate—and those which don't. They should face their problems as mature adults . . . calmly and confidently. There is something magical to be found is such soothing conversation; tensions and anxieties are reduced when they find verbal expression. To the men of the world, I can only say, "Try it."[6]

Would you say that *most* marital problems are caused by sexual difficulties?
No, the opposite is more accurate. Most sexual problems are caused by marital difficulties. Or stated another way, marital conflicts occurring *in bed* are usually caused by marital conflicts occurring *out of bed*.[7]

My wife rarely experiences orgasms, and yet she says she enjoys our sexual relationship. Is this possible?
Many wives, like yours, can participate fully in sexual relations and feel satisfied at the conclusion even though there is no convulsing, ecstatic climax to the episode. (Other, more sensual women feel tremendous frustration if the tension and the vascular engorgement are not discharged.) The important thing is that a husband not *demand* that his wife experience orgasms, and he should certainly not insist that they occur simultaneously with his. To do this is to ask for the impossible, and it puts a woman in an unresolvable conflict. When the husband insists that his wife's orgasms be part of *his* enjoyment, she has but three choices: (1) She can lose interest in sex altogether, as happens with constant failure in any activity; (2) She can try and try and try—and cry; or (3) She can "fake it." Once a woman begins to bluff in bed, there is no place to stop. Forever after, she must make her husband think she's on a prolonged pleasure trip, when in fact her car is still in the garage.

An important key to a satisfactory sex life is to take it as you find it, and enjoy it the way it is. Attempting to meet some arbitrary standard or conform to the testimonials of others is a certain road to frustration.[8]

You stated on one of your television programs that the sexual revolution has resulted in a higher incidence of certain physical problems. Explain what you mean.
I was discussing that observation with my guest, the late Dr. David Hernandez, an obstetrician and gynecologist from the University of Southern California School of Medicine. He had noted an increase in the presence of the disorders which are known to be "soft spots" for emotional pressures— gastrointestinal (digestive) disorders, migraine headaches, high blood pressure, colonitis and general fatigue. Dr. Hernandez believed, and I agree, that these medical problems are more prevalent among those who struggle to overcome sexual mediocrity—those who are now under such intense pressure to "perform" in bed. The stress and anxiety that they feel over their orgasmic inadequacies actually affects their physical health adversely.

Incidentally, Dr. Hernandez commented further that many

men and women engage in sexual intercourse for reasons which God never intended. He listed a few of those illicit motives:

1. Sex is often permitted as a marital duty.
2. It is offered to repay or secure a favor.
3. It represents conquest or victory.
4. It stands as a substitute for verbal communication.
5. It is used to overcome feelings of inferiority (especially in men who seek proof of their masculinity).
6. It is an enticement for emotional love (especially by women who use their bodies to obtain masculine attention).
7. It is a defense against anxiety and tension.
8. It is provided or withheld in order to manipulate the partner.
9. It is engaged in for the purpose of bragging to others.

These "non-loving" reasons for participating in the sex act rob it of meaning and reduce it to an empty and frustrating social game. Sexual intercourse in marriage should bring pleasure, of course, but it should also provide a method of communicating a very deep spiritual commitment. Women are typically more sensitive to this need.[9]

You have said that the sexual revolution has the power to destroy us as a people. On what evidence do you base that supposition?
Mankind has known intuitively for at least fifty centuries that indiscriminate sexual activity represented both an individual and a corporate threat to survival. The wisdom of those years has now been documented. Anthropologist J. D. Unwin conducted an exhaustive study of the eighty-eight civilizations which have existed in the history of the world. Each culture has reflected a similar life cycle, beginning with a strict code of sexual conduct and ending with the demand for complete "freedom" to express individual passion. Unwin reports that *every* society which extended sexual permissiveness to its people was soon to perish. There have been no exceptions.[10]

Why do you think the sexual behavior of a people is related to the strength and stability of their nation? I don't see how those factors are connected.

Sex and survival are linked because the energy which holds a people together is sexual in nature! The physical attraction between men and women causes them to establish a family and invest themselves in its development. It is this force which encourages them to work and save and toil to insure the survival of their families. This sexual energy provides the impetus for the raising of healthy children and for the transfer of values from one generation to the next. It urges a man to work when he would rather play. It causes a woman to save when she would rather spend. In short, the sexual aspect of our nature—when released exclusively within the family—produces stability and responsibility that would not otherwise occur. When a nation is composed of millions of devoted, responsible family units, the entire society is stable and responsible and resilient.

Conversely, the indiscriminate release of sexual energy outside the boundaries of the family is potentially catastrophic. The very force which binds a people together then becomes the agent for its own destruction. Perhaps this point can be illustrated by an analogy between sexual energy in the nuclear family and physical energy in the nucleus of a tiny atom. Electrons, neutrons, and protons are held in delicate balance by an electrical force within each atom. But when that atom and its neighbors are split in nuclear fission (as in an atomic bomb), the energy which had provided the internal stability is then released with unbelievable power and destruction. There is ample reason to believe that this comparison between the nucleus of an atom and the nuclear family is more than incidental.

Who can deny that a society is seriously weakened when the intense sexual urge between men and women becomes an instrument for suspicion and intrigue within millions of individual families . . . when a woman never knows what her husband is doing when away from home . . . when a husband can't trust his wife in his absence . . . when half of the brides are pregnant at the altar . . . when each newlywed has slept with numerous partners, losing the exclusive wonder of the marital bed . . . when everyone is doing his own thing, particularly that which brings him immediate sensual gratification? Unfortunately, the most devastated victim of an immoral society of this nature is the vulnerable little child who hears his parents scream and argue; their tension and frustrations spill over into his world, and the instability of his home leaves its ugly scars on his young mind. Then he watches his parents separate in anger, and he says, "good-bye" to the father he needs and loves. Or perhaps we should speak of the thousands of babies born to unmarried teenage mothers each year, many of whom will never know the meaning of a warm, nurturing home. Or maybe we should discuss the rampant scourge of venereal disease which has reached epidemic proportions among America's youth. This is the true vomitus of the sexual revolution, and I am tired of hearing it romanticized and glorified. God has clearly forbidden irresponsible sexual behavior, not to deprive us of fun and pleasure, but to spare us the disastrous consequences of this festering way of life. Those individuals, and those nations, which choose to defy His commandments on this issue will pay a dear price for their folly.[11]

How common is the *desire* for extramarital sexual encounters in men, even among those who would never be unfaithful to their wives?
Dr. Robert Whitehurst, from the Department of Sociology at the University of Windsor, Ontario, was once asked this question: "Do most men, at some point, have extramarital desires?" His reply, published in the journal, *Sexual Behavior*, included these comments: " . . . *All* men from the first day of marriage onward *think* about this possibility . . . *Although* these tendencies toward extramarital sexual activity diminish in later middle age and beyond, they never entirely vanish or disappear in normal men."

These strong statements leave little room for exceptions, but I'm inclined to agree with their conclusions. The lure of infidelity has incredible power to influence human behavior. Even Christian men, who are committed to God and their wives, must deal with the same sexual temptations. Nevertheless, the Apostle Peter wrote in unmistakable terms about people who yield to these pressures: "With eyes full of adultery, they never stop sinning; they seduce the unstable; they are experts in greed—an accursed brood! *They have left the straight way* and wandered off to follow the way of Balaam son of Beor, who loved the wages of wickedness" (2 Pet. 2:14, 15 NIV, emphasis added).[12]

**If we are to believe the statistics we read today, infidelity
has become extremely common in the Western culture.
Why do people do it? What is the *primary* motivator that
would cause a husband or wife to "cheat"—to even risk
destroying their homes and families for an illicit affair?**
Every situation is different, of course, but I have observed the
most powerful influence to emanate from *ego needs.* Both men
and women appear equally vulnerable to this consuming desire
to be admired and respected by members of the opposite sex.
Therefore, those who become entangled in an affair often do so
because they want to prove that they are still attractive to
women (or men). The thrill comes from knowing "someone
finds me sexy, or intelligent, or pretty or handsome. That
person enjoys hearing me talk . . . likes the way I think . . . finds
me exciting." These feelings flow from the core of the
personality—the ego—and they can make a sane man or
woman behave in foolish and dishonorable ways.

I'm reminded of the seventh chapter of Proverbs, wherein
King Solomon is warning young men not to patronize
prostitutes. These are the words of Israel's wisest king:

> I was looking out the window of my house one day, and saw
> a simple-minded lad, a young man lacking common sense,
> walking at twilight down the street to the house of this
> wayward girl, a prostitute. She approached him, saucy and
> pert, and dressed seductively. She was the brash, coarse
> type, seen often in the streets and markets, soliciting at
> every corner for men to be her lovers.
>
> She put her arms around him and kissed him, and with a
> saucy look she said, "I've decided to forget our quarrel! I
> was just coming to look for you and here you are! My bed is
> spread with lovely, colored sheets of finest linen imported
> from Egypt, perfumed with myrrh, aloes and cinnamon.
> Come on, let's take our fill of love until morning, for my
> husband is away on a long trip. He has taken a wallet full of
> money with him, and won't return for several days."
>
> So she seduced him with her pretty speech, her coaxing
> and her wheedling, until he yielded to her. *He couldn't
> resist her flattery.* He followed her as an ox going to the
> butcher, or as a stag that is trapped, waiting to be killed
> with an arrow through its heart. He was as a bird flying
> into a snare, not knowing the fate awaiting it there.

Listen to me, young men, and not only listen but obey; don't let your desires get out of hand; don't let yourself think about her. Don't go near her; stay away from where she walks, lest she tempt you and seduce you. For she has been the ruin of multitudes—a vast host of men have been her victims. If you want to find the road to hell, look for her house (Prov. 7:6-27 TLB, *emphasis added*).

The key phrase in Solomon's description is found in the italicized words above: "He couldn't resist her flattery." While the sexual motive was evident, he finally fell victim to his own ego needs. Millions have done likewise![13]

How about the desire for sex, itself. Does it play an equally influential role in motivating infidelity among men and women?

It is risky to generalize, because human beings reveal such wide diversity in sexuality from person to person. I believe, however, that unfaithful men are typically more interested in the excitation of sexual intercourse, and women are more motivated by emotional involvement. This is why a woman often gets hurt in such an encounter, because the man loses interest in their relationship when his mistress ceases to stimulate him as before. Someone wrote, "Men love women in proportion to their strangeness to them." Although the word "love" is used inappropriately in that proverb, there is a grain of truth in its message.[14]

You have been in a position to observe those who get involved in affairs in order to deal with their unmet needs. What happens to them? If we checked in on them two or three years later, what would be found?

I have carefully watched such people who have left the world of responsibility—the "straight life"—and have observed a virtual inevitability. These individuals eventually establish another "straight life." The grass is greener on the other side of the fence, but it still has to be mowed. Sooner or later, the pleasure of an illicit affair has to come to an end. Folks have to get back to work. Nor can the fantastic romantic feeling last forever. In fact, the new lover soon becomes rather commonplace, just like the former husband or wife. His or her flaws come into focus, and the couple has their first fight. That takes the edge off the thrill. And the sexual relationship gradually loses its breathtaking quality because it's no longer new. There are times when it doesn't appeal at all. But most significantly, the man and woman eventually turn their thoughts to earning a living and cooking and cleaning and paying taxes again, permitting ego needs to accumulate as before. Alas, after the emotions have been on a moon-shot, they are destined to come back down to earth once more.

Then what does our amorous couple do when they conclude for the second time that the straight life has become intolerably heavy? I am acquainted with men and women, and so are you, who have ripped from one straight life to another in vain search of prolonged pleasure and sex- and ego-gratification. In so doing, they leave in their wake former husbands or wives who feel rejected and bitter and unloved. They produce little children who crave the affection of a father or mother . . . but never find it. All that is left on the march toward old age is a series of broken relationships and shattered lives and hostile children. A scriptural principle foretells the inevitable outcome: "Then when lust hath conceived, it bringeth forth sin: and sin, when it is finished, bringeth forth death" (Jas. 1:15 KJV).[15]

Have you found in your counseling practice that even professing Christians are being caught in the trap of marital infidelity?
It's extremely naive, I think, to believe that those who call themselves Christians are not affected by the moral depravity of our times. Outside of hunger, the most powerful of all human urges and drives is the sexual appetite. Christians are also influenced by the same biochemical forces within their bodies as are non-Christians. I find that Satan can sometimes use this as a tool against us when other temptations do not work, because the sexual desire becomes intertwined with our natural need for love, acceptance, belonging, caring, and tenderness. The trap is laid, and many Christians are falling into it, just like those outside the Christian community.[16]

It is my understanding that some women fail to enjoy sex because of weakness of the muscular structure in the pelvic region. Is this true? What can be done about it?

The late Dr. Arnold Kegel, professor of obstetrics and gynecology at USC School of Medicine, accumulated considerable evidence to show that sexual response is inhibited in women whose pubococcygeal muscle was flaccid. He offered simple exercises to tone up the muscle, and reported remarkable results from women who had previously been inorgasmic. There are other causes for sexual dysfunction, obviously, but for women who are interested in learning more about this physical explanation, I suggest they read *The Act of Marriage* by Tim LaHaye (Zondervan).[17]

Would you express your opinion on the matter of abortion on demand? How do you see the moral issues involved, especially from a Christian perspective?
I have considered the abortion issue from every vantage point and now I find myself absolutely and unequivocally opposed to "abortion on demand." There were many considerations which led to this position, including the impact of abortions on our perception of human life. It is interesting to note, for example, that a woman who plans to terminate her pregnancy usually refers to the life within her as "the fetus." But if she intends to deliver and love and care for the little child, she affectionately calls him "my baby." The need for this distinction is obvious: If we are going to kill a human being without experiencing guilt, we must first strip it of worth and dignity. We must give it a clinical name that denies its personhood. That has been so effectively accomplished in our society that an unborn child during his first six months in gestation can now be sacrificed with no sense of loss on anyone's part. There would be a far greater public outcry if we were destroying puppies or kittens than there is for the million abortions that occur in America each year. Psychiatrist Thomas Szasz reflects the casualness with which we have accepted these deaths by writing, "[abortions] should be available in the same way as, say, an operation for beautification of the nose."

I agree with Francis Schaeffer that the changing legal attitudes toward abortions carry major implications for human life at all levels. If the rights of an unborn child can be sacrificed by reinterpretation by the Supreme Court, why could not other unnecessary people be legislated out of existence? For example, the expense and inconvenience of caring for the severely retarded could easily lead to the same social justification that has encouraged us to kill the unborn (i.e., they will be an expensive nuisance if permitted to live). And how about getting rid of the very old members of our population who contribute nothing to society? And why should we allow deformed infants to live, etc? Perhaps the reader feels those chilling possibilities would never materialize, but I'm not so sure. We already live in a society where some patients will kill an unborn child if they determine through amniocentesis that its sex is not the one they desired.

There are many other aspects of the abortion issue that underscore its inherent evil, but the most important evidence for me came from the Scripture. Of course, the Bible does not address itself directly to the practice of abortions. However, I was amazed to observe how many references are made in both the Old and New Testaments to God's personal acquaintance with children prior to birth. Not only is He aware of their gestations but He is specifically knowledgeable of them as unique individuals and personalities.

Consider the following examples:

1. The angel Gabriel said of John the Baptist, "and he shall be filled with the Holy Ghost, *even from his mother's womb*" (Luke 1:15 KJV, emphasis added).

2. The prophet Jeremiah wrote about himself, "The Lord said to me, I knew you *before* you were formed within your mother's womb; *before you were born* I sanctified you and appointed you as my spokesman to the world' " (Jer. 1:4, 5 TLB, emphasis added).

These two individuals were hardly inhuman embryos before their birth. They were already known to the Creator, who had assigned them a life's work by divine decree.

3. In the book of Genesis we are told that

Isaac pleaded with Jehovah to give Rebekah a child, for even after many years of marriage she had no children. Then at last she became pregnant. And it seemed as though children were fighting each other inside her!

"I can't endure this," she exclaimed. So she asked the Lord about it.

And he told her, "The sons in your womb shall become two rival nations. One will be stronger than the other; and the older shall be the servant of the younger!" (Gen. 25:21-23 TLB).

Again, God was aware of the developing personalities in these unborn twins and foretold their future conflicts. The mutual hatred of their descendants is still evident in the Middle East today.

4. Jesus Himself was conceived by the Holy Spirit, which fixes God's involvement with Christ from the time He was a single cell inside Mary's uterus. (See Matt. 1:18.)

5. The most dramatic example, however, is found in the 139th Psalm. King David describes his own prenatal relationship with God, which is stunning in its impact.

You made all the delicate, inner parts of my body, and knit them together in my mother's womb. Thank you for making me so wonderfully complex! It is amazing to think about. Your workmanship is marvelous—and how well I know it. You were there while I was being formed in utter seclusion! You saw me before I was born and scheduled each day of my life before I began to breathe. Every day was recorded in your Book! (Psa. 139:13-16 TLB).

That passage is thrilling to me, because it implies that God not only scheduled each day of David's life, but He did the same for *me*. He was there when *I* was being formed in utter seclusion, and He personally made all the delicate inner parts of *my* body. Imagine that! The Great Creator of the universe lovingly supervised my development during those preconscious days *in utero,* as He did for every human being on earth. Surely, anyone who can grasp that concept without sensing an exhilaration is stone-cold dead! From my point of view, these scriptural references absolutely refute the notion that unborn children do not have a soul or personhood until they are born at full term. I can't believe it! No rationalization can justify detaching a healthy little human being from his place of safety and leaving him to suffocate on a porcelain table. No social or financial considerations can counter-balance our collective guilt for destroying those lives which were being fashioned in the image of God Himself. Throughout the Gospels, Jesus revealed a tenderness toward boys and girls ("Suffer little children to come unto me"), and some of His most frightening warnings were addressed to those who would hurt them. It is my deepest conviction that He will not hold us blameless for our wanton infanticide. As He said to Cain, who killed Abel, "Your brother's blood calls to me from the ground!"

Surely, other Christians have drawn the same conclusion. I must ask, where are those moral leaders who agree with me? Why have pastors and ministers been so timid and mute on this vital matter? It is time that the Christian church found its tongue and spoke in defense of the unborn children who are unable to plead for their own lives.[18]

SECTION 8
HOMO-SEXUALITY

What causes homosexuality?
Homosexuality has many causes, in the same way that a fever
may occur from different sources. However, as a generalization,
it can be said that homosexuality often seems to result from an
unhappy home life, usually involving confusion in sexual
identity.[1]

**What is the most common home environment of a future
homosexual?**
Again, conditions vary tremendously, and any generalization
offered can be contradicted by numerous exceptions. If there is
a common thread, it seems to be a home where the mother is
dominating, overprotective, and possessive, while the father is
rejecting and ridiculing of the child. The opposite situation
occurs, too, where the mother rejects her son because he is a
male. There are other cases where homosexuality occurs in a
seemingly happy home where no obvious distortion in parent
roles can be observed. I must stress that there are many
hypotheses (guesses) about the origins of this perversion, but
absolute conclusions are still not available.[2]

**What can parents do to prevent homosexuality in their
children?**
The best prevention is to strengthen their home life.
Homosexuality can occur in a loving home, as indicated,
although it is less likely where parents are reasonably well
adjusted to one another. I don't think it is necessary to fear this

unfortunate occurrence as a force beyond our control. If parents will provide a healthy, stable home environment, and not interfere with the child's appropriate sex role, then homosexuality is highly unlikely to occur in the younger set.[3]

What should be the Christian's attitude toward homosexuality?

I believe our obligation is to despise the sin but love the sinner. Many men and women who experience homosexual passions have not sought their way of life; it occurred for reasons which they can neither recall nor explain. Some were victims of early traumatic sexual encounters by adults who exploited them. I remember one homosexual teenager whose drunken father forced him to sleep with his mother after a wild New Year's Eve party. His disgust for heterosexual sex was easy to trace. Such individuals need acceptance and love from the Christian community, as they seek to redirect their sexual impulses.

On the other hand, I cannot justify the revisionist view of Scripture which would interpret homosexuality as just another lifestyle available to the Christian. The divinely inspired biblical writers would not have referred to homosexuality with such abhorrence if it were not an evil practice in the eyes of God. Whenever this perversion is mentioned in the New Testament, it is listed with the most heinous of sins and misbehaviors. For example, Paul wrote in 1 Corinthians 6:9, 10:

> Don't you know that the wicked will not inherit the kingdom of God? Do not be deceived: Neither the sexually immoral nor idolaters nor adulterers nor male prostitutes nor homosexual offenders nor thieves nor the greedy nor drunkards nor slanderers nor swindlers will inherit the kingdom of God (NIV).

Romans 1:26, 27 describes God's attitude toward homosexuality in equally unmistakable terms:

> Because of this, God gave them over to shameful lusts. Even their women exchanged natural relations for unnatural ones. In the same way the men also abandoned natural relations with women and were inflamed with lust for one another. Men committed indecent acts with other men, and received in themselves the due penalty for their perversion (NIV).

What is the responsibility, then, of the person who wants to be a Christian but struggles with a deeply ingrained attraction to members of his or her own sex?
If I interpret Scripture properly, that person is obligated to subject his sexual desires to the same measure of self-control that heterosexual single adults must exercise. In other words, he must refrain from the expression of his lusts. I know that it is easier to write about this self-discipline than to implement it, but we are promised in Scripture, "God is faithful, and he will not let you be tempted beyond your strength, but with the temptation will also provide the way of escape, that you may be able to endure it" (1 Cor. 10:13 RSV).

Second, I would recommend that the homosexual enter into a therapeutic relationship with a *Christian* psychologist or psychiatrist who is equally committed to Christian virtues. This condition *can* be treated successfully when the individual wants to be helped, and when a knowledgeable professional is dedicated to the same goal. Some of my colleagues report better than a 70 percent "cure" rate when these conditions exist ("cure" being defined as the individual becoming comfortable in a heterosexual relationship and making at least a moderately successful adjustment to a non-homosexual lifestyle).

What is bisexuality and why are we hearing so much about it now?
A bisexual is someone who participates in both heterosexual and homosexual acts of passion. Since the mid-seventies, bisexuality has been a fad among swingers and has received enormous amounts of publicity in the American press. The cover of a *Cosmopolitan* magazine posed the question, "Is Bisexuality Thinkable (or Even Do-able) for Non-nut Cases?" Inside, the caption read, "Could *you* be ready for a lesbian encounter? Well, a surprising number of perfectly 'normal' man-loving females are—." The article concluded with this statement: "Whether or not we're all predestined to be bisexual remains in question. Still, whatever happens in the future, I've concluded that, right now, for the many who've tried it, bisexuality offers a satisfying—and often loving—way of life."[4]

Vogue magazine carried a similar feature story with the same message. Alex Comfort, writing in *More Joy,* predicted that bisexuality will be the standard, middle-class morality within ten years.

These immoral "prophets" remind me of the eternal words of another prophet named Isaiah, writing in the Old Testament. He said, "Woe unto them that call evil good, and good evil; that put darkness for light, and light for darkness; that put bitter for sweet, and sweet for bitter! . . . Therefore, as the fire devoureth the stubble, and as the flame consumeth the chaff, so their root shall be as rottenness, and their blossom shall go up as dust: because they have cast away the law of the Lord of hosts, and despised the word of the Holy One of Israel" (Isa. 5:20, 24).

Morality and immorality are not defined by man's changing attitudes and social customs. They are determined by the God of the universe, whose timeless standards cannot be ignored with impunity![5]

SECTION 9
COPING WITH MENOPAUSE

Our children are all on their own now and my husband and
I are free to do some of the traveling we have always
planned to do when we got them through college. But
lately I feel too tired even to keep the house clean, and too
depressed to care about planning anything extra. Some
days I can hardly get out of bed in the morning. I just want
to put my head under the pillow and cry—for no reason at
all. So why do I feel so terrible? My husband is trying to
be patient, but this morning he growled, "You have
everything a woman could want . . . what do *you* have to
be blue about?" Do you think I could be losing my mind?
I think it is quite unlikely that you have anything wrong with
your mind. The symptoms you describe sound as if you may be
entering a physiological phase called menopause, and your
discomfort may be caused by the hormonal imbalance that
accompanies glandular upheaval. I suggest that you make an
appointment to see a gynecologist in the next few days.

Can you give me a simple definition of menopause?
It is a period of transition in a woman's life when the
reproductive capacity is phasing out and her body is
undergoing the many chemical and psychological changes
associated with that cessation. Menstruation, which has
occurred monthly since perhaps eleven or twelve years of age,
now gradually stops, and hormonal readjustments occur.
Specifically, the ovaries produce only about one-eighth the
estrogen that they once did. This affects not only the
reproductive system, but the body's entire physical and
psychological apparatus.[1]

Do all women feel as miserable as I do when menopause occurs?
It is estimated that approximately 85 percent of women go through menopause without major disruption in their daily lives. They may experience distressing symptoms for a time, but they are able to function and cope with the responsibilities of living. The remaining 15 percent, however, experience much more serious difficulties. Some are completely immobilized by the chemical changes occurring within.[2]

What are the primary symptoms of hormone imbalance during menopause?
I will list them, although I must caution you to understand that other physical and emotional problems can also produce the same or similar difficulties. Furthermore, this list is not complete. Menopausal physiology can be expressed in a wide variety of symptoms, varying in intensity.

Emotional Symptoms
1. Extreme depression, perhaps lasting for months without relief.
2. Extremely low self-esteem, bringing feelings of utter worthlessness and disinterest in living.
3. Extremely low frustration tolerance, giving rise to outbursts of temper and emotional ventilation.
4. Inappropriate emotional responses, producing tears when things are not sad and depression during relatively good times.
5. Low tolerance to noise. Even the sound of a radio or the normal responses of children can be extremely irritating. Ringing in the ears is also common.
6. Great needs for proof of love are demanded, and in their absence, suspicion of a rival may be hurled at the husband.
7. Interferences with sleep patterns.
8. Inability to concentrate and difficulty in remembering.

Physical Symptoms
1. Gastrointestinal disorders, interfering with digestion and appetite.
2. "Hot flashes" which burn in various parts of the body for a few seconds.
3. Vertigo (dizziness).

4. Constipation.
5. Trembling.
6. Hands and feet tingle and "go to sleep."
7. Dryness of the skin, especially in specific patches in various places, and loss of elasticity.
8. Dryness of the mucous membranes, especially in the vagina, making intercourse painful or impossible.
9. Greatly reduced libido (sexual desire).
10. Pain in various joints of the body, shifting from place to place (neuralgias, myalgias and arthralgias).
11. Tachycardia (accelerated or racing heartbeat) and palpitation.
12. Headaches.
13. Dark, gloomy circles around the eyes. (This is the symptom which I have found most useful in preliminary diagnosis.)
14. Loss of weight.

For the besieged woman who staggers into her physician's office with most of these symptoms, her condition has facetiously been called "The falling hand syndrome." She points to her left eyebrow and says, "Oh! My head has been splitting, and my ears have this funny ringing, and my breasts hurt and oh! My stomach is killing me; and I've got this pain in my lower back, and my buttocks hurt and my knee is quivering." Truly, her hand tumbles inch by inch from the top of her crown to the bottom of her aching feet. A physician told me recently that his nurse was attempting to obtain a medical history from such a woman who answered affirmatively to every possible disorder. Whatever disease or problem she mentioned, the patient professed to have had it. Finally in exasperation, the nurse asked if her teeth itched, just to see what the patient would say. The woman frowned for a moment, then ran her tongue over her front teeth and said, "Come to think of it, they sure do!" A menopausal woman such as this is likely to think *everything* has gone wrong.[3]

When I was young, my mother told me that menopause happens when a woman is about forty-five. I'm having some of the symptoms you have described, but I'm only thirty-seven. Surely I'm too young for menopause, don't you think?

The age of onset of menopause varies widely. It can occur at *any* adult age—as early as the twenties or as late as the fifties. As your mother indicated, the early forties represent the mid-range, but individuals differ significantly.[4]

I am going through menopause now. The things you have said about the causes of my uncomfortable symptoms are very helpful, and I really understand myself better now. But what I want to know is, "Will this ever end? Will I feel like my old self again someday?"
There is definitely a silver lining to the dark cloud that hangs over you now! The experience is not a permanent state, but a stage of a journey through which some women must go. But "this too shall pass." It may last for several years, but *it will pass.* Just as with men in mid-life crisis, the period after menopause can be brighter, happier, more stable and more healthy than any other period of life. Often, a more balanced personality develops after menopause and greater energy is experienced. A better day *is* coming!

Incidentally, the human female is the only member of the animal kingdom who outlives its reproductive capacity by a significant period of time. (Does that help your self-esteem?)[5]

Why do some women make it through menopause without the need for estrogen replacement therapy?
I don't think anyone can answer that question, because no one knows for sure what estrogen does to the feminine neurological apparatus. Perhaps the ovaries or the adrenal glands emit enough estrogen to satisfy the needs of a less vulnerable individual. At this point, little is known about the chemistry of the brain and the substances which are necessary for its proper functioning. The guide in treatment then, is the clinical signs and symptoms which the physician observes.[6]

Is there a "male menopause" comparable to what is experienced by women?
This is a question with strong cultural overtones which have clouded the truth. Some women apparently fear that female mcnopause will be used as an excuse to withhold positions of leadership from middle-aged women. Therefore, they stress the existence of a comparable "male menopause." While men do

experience a climacteric which can be called menopausal, it is very different in origin and impact from that experienced by women. For men, the changes are not so related to hormonal alterations but are more psychological in nature. It is difficult for a man to face the fact that he will never reach the occupational goals that he set for himself . . . that his youth is rapidly vanishing . . . that he will soon be unattractive to the opposite sex . . . that his earlier dreams of glory and power will never be realized. Some men who have achieved less than they hoped are devastated by the realization that life is slipping away from them. This, primarily, is the male menopause. Some individuals respond to it by seeking an affair with a young girl to prove their continued virility; others become alcoholics; still others enter into dramatic periods of depression. But even when the emotional impact is extreme, it is usually motivated by the man's evaluation of his outside world. These same influences agitate a woman, but she has an additional hormonal turmoil undermining her security from within. Other things being equal, the feminine variety is more difficult to endure, particularly if it remains untreated.[7]

Dr. Dobson's note: In January 1982 the Focus on the Family radio broadcast featured a series of interviews between myself and Southern California physician, Dr. Paul Chapman, on the subject of hormone imbalance—its symptoms and treatments.

As a companion to that series, Focus on the Family offered the following article which was brought to our attention by our guest-physician. Although it was originally published in 1963, Dr. Chapman feels the content of this article continues to represent the most concise and accurate explanation available on the subject of hormone imbalance in mid-life.

Notably missing from the article, of course, is any reference to the more recent controversy that has arisen over the use of estrogen replacement therapy (ERT). Several medical articles published during the mid-seventies served to validate the suspicion that prolonged and indiscriminate use of ERT seemed to be related to cancer of the uterus in some women. However, physicians remain divided on the risks involved in the careful, monitored use of the hormone. There are those, including Dr. Chapman, who believe that the consequences of not providing ERT to a woman who desperately needs it are more threatening than are the known risks of its use. Other physicians are philosophically opposed to estrogen replacement therapy in any instance.

Further gynecological investigations are currently
underway in medical centers around the country. In the
absence of definitive conclusions at this time, it is
recommended that women with menopausal symptoms
seek and accept the counsel of their physicians.

HORMONE IMBALANCE IN MID-LIFE
by Lawrence Galton

A profound change now taking place in medical thinking could
affect the life of millions of women—in fact, of virtually every
woman.

"In my practice the menopause is a disease process, requiring
active intervention." In these emphatic words Dr. Allan C.
Barnes, chairman of the department of obstetrics and
gynecology at Johns Hopkins University School of Medicine,
has stated a revolutionary new concept now held by a growing
number of leading gynecologists. It is a concept of importance
to all women—and especially to younger women.

The concept is based on mounting evidence that—whether it
comes as early as age thirty-five (as it does for some women) or
as late as age fifty-five (as it does for some others)—the decline of
the ovaries that brings on "change of life" can have more than
a temporary impact. There can be serious, previously
unappreciated consequences for the rest of a woman's life:

- This decline in ovarian function can take away from a
  woman many of her prized feminine attributes, changing
  the appearance of her body and even to some extent
  masculinizing it.
- The decline can produce many degenerative or irritative
  changes within her body.
- After menopause a woman may become prone, as she was
  not earlier, to heart disease and painful bone disease.
- The menopause can lead to a rapid decline in a woman's
  mental functioning—to an acceleration of her intellectual
  and psychological aging as well as her physical aging.

But this gloomy picture fortunately has a brighter side.
There is evidence that these consequences need not be
inevitable—that, if women are alert to them and seek help for
them, they can often be overcome. And if young women are
alert to them and seek help early enough, the consequences can
often be prevented.

Indeed, the promise is that for young women a whole new era

of preventive medicine is at hand; for them, a diminishing return from life is not something to be listlessly expected but something to be actively avoided.

The new concept says, in effect, that menopause can be a deficiency disease—just as diabetes is a deficiency disease and hypothyroidism is a deficiency disease—and deficiency can be made up for the menopause just as it can be made up for other disorders.

The Case of the Frantic Pituitary. This concept developed because doctors have in recent years been devoting a great deal of study to the obvious symptoms of the menopause and also to other effects that have been not so obvious at all.

The obvious symptoms are the acute ones about which every woman has heard *ad nauseam.* The classic ill-famed one is the hot flash, a sudden sensation of heat that sweeps over the body to the head, producing an intense flushing of the face that is often followed by profuse sweating and cold shivering. Others include headache, weakness, palpitation, insomnia, and dizziness.

Often there are emotional difficulties. "It is as if the color of the lenses through which a woman sees the world were changed from rose to blue," one physician has said. "She becomes anxious, apprehensive, depressed, melancholic, irritable, and emotionally unstable."

What causes such disturbances?

Even as recently as two generations ago there was no basic understanding. Until the 1920s no one knew that the ovaries produce estrogen. Since that time it has become clear that it is this hormone that shapes a girl into a woman and permits her to bear children. The decline of the ovaries and of their estrogen production brings on menopause and, in doing so, grinds menstruation to a halt. But the ovarian decline can also produce upsets for other glands. The picture is this:

All through their active years the ovaries secrete estrogen under the command of the pituitary. The pituitary, master gland of the body at the base of the brain, also commands other important endocrine glands, including the thyroid and the adrenals. When at menopause the ovaries no longer are able to respond adequately to its order, the pituitary becomes disturbed. Its control over other glands is affected, and the result may be hormonal imbalance that affects the whole nervous system.

More Than a "Brief Transition." Not all women have great
difficulty with acute menopausal symptoms. Actually, the
decline in ovarian production during the aging process has
extreme variation—and this is the reason there is such wide
variation in the age at which menopause arrives.

When it does arrive, the ovaries may not shut down
completely but may continue to secrete some estrogen; the
adrenal glands atop the kidneys also produce some. The total
varies from one woman to another. And so do the symptoms.

Thus, in one study covering 1,000 women, 50.8 percent were
found to have no acute discomfort. Of those who experienced
difficulties, 89.7 percent could work as usual without
interruption; only 10.3 percent were truly incapacitated at
intervals.

Treatment has in the past been largely conservative. The
principle has been that "change of life" is simply a period of
adjustment that may last from a few months to a year or
two—till the body has a chance to become attuned to the new
situation in which the ovaries no longer play their once-active
role in the physical economy.

Reassurance has been a major part of therapy. The thought
has been that women can, by understanding that menopause is
a passing phase and any discomforts will before long disappear,
go through the adjustment period much more easily. And the
fact is that many have been relieved to a considerable extent of
nervous and emotional disturbances and even of hot flashes by
simple reassurance from a doctor in whom they have faith and
who has been willing to take the time to provide reassurance.

In more severe cases estrogen has been used. The objective
has been to employ it briefly, to use just enough to quiet the
excited pituitary, and gradually to taper off the doses to help the
body reach a new balance in easy stages—in short, to smooth
the transition.

But of late there has been increasing evidence that there is
much more to be considered than a short transition—that the
ovaries, through their secretion of estrogen, have many roles
beyond that of making reproduction possible and that their
decline can have wide repercussions for the rest of a woman's
life.

A Key to Broken Hips and Heart Attacks. One of the most
striking—and potentially serious—consequences of estrogen
decline is loss of protection against heart trouble.

Recent studies have been showing that hardening and narrowing of the arteries that feed the heart, a major cause of heart attacks, is as much as ten times more prevalent in men under age forty than in women of similar age. But after menopause the picture changes, and women as a group become equally prone to develop coronary disease. Estrogen, it seems, is a major factor in keeping down the blood levels of cholesterol and other fats that in excess are associated with *atherosclerosis,* the hardening and narrowing of the coronary arteries. With the decline of ovarian-estrogen production a woman loses her favored status.

Another common aftermath of that decline is *osteoporosis,* a thinning of the bone structure. Estrogen has an influence on protein balance. With lower levels of the hormone, protein may be lost from bone, and calcium depletion may follow.

One frequent symptom of osteoporosis is chronic back pain. Osteoporosis may also weaken the bones enough so that they tend to break or to collapse more easily. "The eighty-year-old woman who suffers a fractured hip," says Dr. Barnes, "can blame it to some extent on the fact that her ovaries ceased functioning thirty years earlier." And fractures of other bones—in the wrists and ribs—often occur after mild injury.

Often, too, bones in the spinal column become compressed so that height is lost. And the spine may also develop an abnormal curvature that leads to the unattractive bent appearance that has come to be called "dowager's hump."

A Loss of Femininity? Estrogen has a great influence also on the *skin*—on its blood supply, elasticity, and other qualities. As ovarian-estrogen output wanes, the skin tends to lose its softness and to become tough, dry, inelastic, and scaly. Some women develop an annoying itch; others are bothered by sensations similar to those produced by insects crawling over the skin.

And there may be masculinization as well. In both men and women both male and female sex hormones are produced. It's the balance that counts. In women the adrenal glands secrete androgen, the male hormone. At menopause they continue to do so, and, with the ovaries producing less estrogen, the balance may be upset enough to cause an increase in facial hair and sometimes a tendency to baldness.

Nor do the effects of estrogen deprivation stop there. It is the increasing supply of estrogen at puberty that brings about breast development, leads to other changes in body contour, and causes the uterus to grow and the vagina to mature. And it is the declining supply at the menopause that leads to reverse changes in all these areas.

Deprived of high levels of the hormone, breasts lose their firmness and tend to become flabby. There is a tendency for fat to be deposited on the hips and upper thighs. The uterus begins to revert to its smaller preadolescent size. The vagina becomes shorter, loses its expandability, and—also because of estrogen deprivation—the lining of the vagina thins and tends to lose its normal acidity.

The loss of acidity may encourage the growth of infectious organisms, and the thinning of the vaginal lining also invites infection. The result is the common problem known as *senile vaginitis,* with its itching, burning, discharge, and sometimes the inability to have marital relations without pain.

Because there is a lymphatic connection between the vagina and the bladder through which infection may spread, vaginitis may lead to *cystitis,* a bladder inflammation that produces urinary urgency and frequency.

For some women there are distressing *arthralgias,* or joint pains. Estrogen deprivation does not, however, foment rheumatoid arthritis (peak incidence occurs before menopause) or osteoarthritis (this tends to increase in severity from late childhood).

Emotional Woes May Develop. As for *emotional upsets,* some physicians now feel that the physical changes occasioned by estrogen deprivation play a more important role than they have been credited with in the past.

True, there can be many other significant factors in bringing about anxiety and depression. Usually, when a woman reaches "the change," her children are grown up and leading their own lives and are no longer in need of her close attention. Her husband may be at the height of his career and preoccupied with it. She may feel less useful—especially if her life has been totally concentrated on her family and if she has no other interests.

Yet, as one physician puts it, "While these factors are disturbing, a mental adjustment for most women would not be too difficult were it not for the physical changes. A woman becomes acutely aware of her loss of physical attractiveness . . . sees the marked skin changes, disfiguring fat deposits, atrophy of her breasts. An irritated or inadequate vagina may bring more unhappiness. All of this has a profound effect upon her psyche."

One Third of a Lifetime . . . All told, the list of possible consequences stemming from the decline of the ovaries is a formidable one, and these consequences have grown in importance as the average life span of women has increased from only forty-eight years at the turn of the century to seventy-five years today. The average woman can expect to live one third of her life (and many women will live half their life) after what in effect amounts to the "death" of the ovaries.

Dr. William H. Masters of Washington University School of Medicine has termed this inability of the ovaries to keep functioning along with other organs "the Achilles' heel of a woman's body." And more and more physicians share his conviction that the medical profession, responsible for adding many years to life, must now face up to doing something about the ovarian-decline problem—"must accept the responsibility of developing effective physiological support."

In 1961 a special report on the status of therapy for the menopause authorized by the American Medical Association's Council on Drugs declared that not just the one to two years of menopause but management of the remaining years of a woman's life "has become the major problem."

How Estrogen Therapy Can Help. There now is evidence from many studies—some carried out over extended periods of time—that the problem can be solved. Estrogen for therapeutic use has been available for more than twenty-five years.

Dr. Stanley Wallach and Dr. Philip H. Hennemann of the Harvard Medical School recently reviewed their records of more than 200 women for whom they prescribed estrogen during the past quarter century:

• Of these women 94 were treated primarily for severe hot flashes that had in many cases been present for three or more years and that had in some cases failed to yield to sedatives and other measures. Estrogen quickly brought relief for 93 of the 94.

• There were 119 other women with severe osteoporosis. Complete relief or great reduction of pain occurred in 90 percent treated with estrogen. Usually pain diminished markedly within two months after start of treatment. A progressive further decrease in discomfort and increase in ability to move freely followed.

- In some of the women osteoporosis had led to losses of height—as much as five inches. Height loss ceased after estrogen was employed.
- And, significantly, in still another group of women, Dr. Wallach and Dr. Hennemann found that when estrogen was started early enough, before osteoporosis could develop, the hormone had a preventive effect. The bone disorder never did develop.

Protection Against Heart Trouble. Estrogen's value for coronary-artery disease—both for treatment and prevention—is being demonstrated increasingly. Physicians have been giving the hormone to women (and to men, as well) who had already experienced a first heart attack. The treatment has markedly reduced the incidence of subsequent attacks and has extended life.

In long-term studies covering more than 200 women, Dr. M. Edward Davis and his associates at the University of Chicago have been investigating estrogen's preventive value. They have reported that, in comparison with other women, those receiving the hormone after menopause have lowered levels of cholesterol and other fats in the blood and also show a lower incidence of the abnormal electrocardiograms that indicate heart trouble. And another gratifying finding has been that women under treatment with estrogen for ten or more years have a lowered incidence of high blood pressure.

Can Other Problems Be Avoided? Doctors have been finding estrogen valuable—sometimes dramatically so—in combating many of the other problems of women during and after menopause.

The hormone is no panacea for the skin and will not restore the bloom of sixteen, but estrogen treatment does greatly improve elasticity and can help to overcome dryness.

In vaginitis, estrogen is remarkably effective, often restoring the vaginal lining to normal within a month and reestablishing vaginal acidity as well. Itching and discharge disappear. Cystitis may also improve.

Many women with joint pains have had gratifying relief with estrogen treatment. And, Dr. Masters has reported, except for the ovaries themselves, all pelvic organs and the breasts are capable of reversing their decline and returning to normal size and function under the influence of estrogen therapy.

Investigators at the Washington University department of

neuropsychiatry have reported studies indicating that estrogen treatment is of some value for intellectual function—that such basic mental processes as memory for recent events, power of definitive thinking, and the ability to absorb new material show some degree of improvement. The amount varies among individuals, but appears to be directly related to the time when treatment is begun—and the earlier treatment is started, the better.

In April, 1963, a medical report, "A Plea for the Maintenance of Adequate Estrogen from Puberty to the Grave," in *The Journal of the American Geriatrics Society* summed up by noting that women in the past *had* to become "stiff, frail, bent, wrinkled, and apathetic . . . they stumbled through their remaining years. The amount and variety of suffering was great. There was little or nothing to do for their skin problems . . . osteoporosis, irritating leucorrheas [vaginal discharge], cracked and bleeding vulvas. It was part of being old. If left to nature, it still is, but most of this suffering can now be prevented and effectively treated."

What Risk of Cancer? Is there any risk in hormone treatment? In the past there has been fear that estrogen might provoke breast or genital cancer. But the 1961 report authorized by the A.M.A.'s Council on Drugs declared that such fear "does not seem justified on the basis of available evidence."

Evidence *against* any such hazard has been coming increasingly from many sources.

For one thing, incidence of cancer at all sites in women increases steadily with age, even as production of estrogen decreases.

For another, investigators have been pointing out that if estrogen provoked cancer, breast cancer should then be encountered frequently in pregnancy because estrogen levels increase greatly, especially in the late months. But breast cancer has been found to be rare in pregnancy.

Studies with animals given large doses of estrogen have revealed no cancer-producing effect—and neither have a number of long-term studies of estrogen treatment in women.

In one study 206 women were treated over a five-and-a-half-year period; no case of cancer developed. In another study covering 120 post-menopausal women treated over an extended period, no cancer was observed, though five to six malignancies were to be expected in that time.

In reporting their twenty-five-year experience with the use of estrogen, Dr. Wallach and Dr. Hennemann of Harvard noted that cancer of the breast was not detected in any patient during prolonged treatment, and only one genital cancer developed. They concluded that "prolonged, cyclic, oral estrogen therapy combined with periodic pelvic and vaginal examinations is a safe and effective therapy."

In 1962 in the *Journal of the American Medical Association* Dr. Robert A. Wilson of the Methodist Hospital of Brooklyn reported on a group of 304 women whose ages ranged from forty to seventy years and who had been treated with estrogens for periods up to twenty-seven years. An estimated eighteen cases of cancer, either breast or genital, he pointed out, would normally have been expected to occur in this number of women. Instead, no cases of cancer were seen.

Far from inducing cancer, Dr. Wilson noted, estrogen may very well have a *preventive* action. "It would seem advisable," he reported, "to keep women endocrine-rich and consequently cancer-poor throughout their lives."

There Are Side Effects. Use of estrogen, however, has not been without problems in the past, and there are some today.

The first compounds were useless when taken by mouth; they had to be injected. Now there are numerous preparations that are effective if taken orally, but they must be used under close medical supervision with careful attention to proper individual dosage.

Some women benefit from very tiny amounts; others require ten times as much. Especially in large amounts, the hormone may provoke irregular bleeding in some women.

Such bleeding is of no importance in itself; it will stop when the drug is withdrawn for a time. But such bleeding clouds the problem of early diagnosis of uterine cancer. Irregular bleeding in the later years can come from not-serious causes, such as polyps, but may also indicate malignancy. And because such malignancy can be cured in its early stages, doctors have learned for safety's sake to consider irregular bleeding as an indication of cancer till definitely proved otherwise.

Trying to avoid the problem of irregular bleeding—and the possible need for curettage to rule out cancer—some doctors use cyclic administration of estrogen and find it effective. They have women take the drug for twenty-five days, stop it for five days, and then resume again—or use another similar schedule of on-and-off treatment.

Some physicians employ a combination of estrogen and androgen, the male sex hormone. And androgen often has another happy effect: It increases the general sense of well-being.

But the estrogen-androgen ratio can be critical. While a ration of twenty units of androgen to one of estrogen has proved valuable for the majority of women, it produces hirsutism, especially growth of facial hair, in about 20 percent. Some physicians have recently been finding that a ten-to-one ratio is effective and greatly reduces the incidence of hirsutism.

It is hoped that pharmaceutical research—now intensive in the hormone field—will before long be able to produce new synthetic compounds that will not have undesirable properties.

A Matter of "Medical Management." Today the big question among gynecologists is just how many women need hormone supplementation.

Some physicians are convinced that every woman should have estrogen treatment not just at menopause but for the rest of life. They feel that other forms of medical management should not be abandoned. Explanation, reassurance, nutritional-and-weight guidance, the use of tranquilizers and other drugs all have their place in individual cases. But these physicians see menopause marking the beginning of a state of estrogen deficiency that demands prolonged estrogen treatment just as diabetes or any other deficiency state demands continued treatment.

Some start treatment after a woman has been free of menses for six months—though estrogen may be employed as early as two months after the last period if a woman complains of hot flashes or other uncomfortable symptoms. And these physicians believe in the need for treatment regardless of whether symptoms are present.

Many other physicians, because there can be great variations in natural estrogen production during and after menopause, are not convinced that treatment should be routine for every woman.

"They do feel, however," says Dr. Edmund Overstreet, professor of obstetrics and gynecology at the University of California, "that approximately 25 percent of post-menopausal women have a true estrogen-deficiency disease that should be supplemented with estrogen therapy for the rest of these women's lives in order to protect them."

All authorities unite in emphasizing one thing—the need for

recognizing that estrogen does not "fix everything." Although it can be valuable in many ways, estrogen is certainly no cure-all. Problems can arise during or after menopause, just as at any other time of life, that have nothing to do with the menopause and for which estrogen is of no value. Careful and regular medical checkups remain vital.

A Test for Estrogen Deficiency. It will take years of experience before the question of whether every woman needs treatment is settled. Better tests could help. Currently the *vaginal smear*—the same test used for cancer detection—can be used to estimate the degree of estrogen deprivation. The smear shows changes in the vaginal lining caused by lack of the hormone and, because the smear also shows beneficial changes when estrogen is given, helps determine the proper dosage. But many physicians feel that more refined and exact tests are needed and will soon be coming.

As of now, most doctors undoubtedly will prefer not to use hormone supplementation routinely but on an individual basis—nor would it be wise for any woman to demand it willy-nilly.

The really important point is this: Every woman can now count on her doctor to take a vigorous interest, more vigorous than ever before, in her progress through and beyond menopause; to be alert to her needs and—with the mounting evidence of its effectiveness and safety—to use hormone treatment, if it seems called for, to make the "change of life" and all the rest of her life healthier and happier. [End of article.]

For the individual who would like to obtain a better understanding of hormone imbalance associated with menopause and premenstrual tension, the following materials can be obtained by writing our non-profit organization, Focus on the Family, Box 500, Arcadia, California 91006.

CASSETTE TAPES:
An Understanding Look at Menopause, Dr. James Dobson ($6.00)
Coping with Premenstrual Tension, Dr. James Dobson ($6.00)
Hormone Imbalance in Mid-Life, Dr. James Dobson and guest, Dr. Paul Chapman ($6.00)

BOOKLETS:
Premenstrual Blues, Dr. Guy Abraham ($.50)
An Understanding Look at Menopause, Dr. James Dobson ($.50)

SECTION 10
MID-LIFE AND BEYOND

Most of your books and talks are directed to younger wives and mothers. But we middle-aged women have problems, too. I've survived most of the stages of life you describe, including menopause, but now I need help in knowing how to grow old gracefully. I don't want to become a boring, sour old woman. Would you offer a few suggestions that will help me avoid some of the problems that are characteristic of post-retirement age?

There are at least four dangers to be circumvented. Let me discuss them briefly.

First, avoid the pitfall of *isolation*. Reuben Welch has written a book entitled, *We Really Do Need Each Other*, and he's absolutely right. Isolation is a bad thing; it ruins the mind. As you grow older, do not allow yourself to withdraw within the four walls of your house and cut yourself off from people. Keep up your social life even when the easiest thing to do is stay at home. Call your friends; they're probably lonely, too. Get involved with people. And remember, loneliness is not something others do to you; it is usually something you do to yourself.

Second, avoid the pitfall of *inactivity*, which is a common trap for the elderly. I once flew into Chicago very late at night and found that the hotel had rented my reserved room to someone else. The manager was obligated to help me find accommodations, but every hotel was full. Finally, he located a room in a facility for the elderly. My brief experience in that converted condominium was enlightening—and depressing. The following morning when I came down to breakfast, I saw four or five hundred elderly people sitting in the huge lobby. Most were silent—neither talking nor interacting. They weren't even reading newspapers. Most were sitting with their heads down, either nodding off to sleep or just staring into space. There was no activity—nor involvement—no interchange between people. How sad it seemed to see so many lonely human beings in one another's company, yet each was lost in his own thoughts. Inactivity and its first cousin, loneliness, are dangerous *enemies* of the elderly.

Third, avoid the pitfall of *self-pity*—an attitude that can kill its victim, quite literally. Those who yield to it are listening to Satan's most vicious lie. Instead of internalizing remorse, I suggest that you begin giving to others: bake something, send flowers, write a card. Get into the world of other people and develop a ministry of prayer for those around you.

Fourth, avoid the pitfall of *despair*. Many elderly people slip into the habit of thinking, "I'm getting old. There's nothing ahead but death . . . life is over." This hopelessness is especially unwarranted for the Christian, who must always be *future-oriented*. The real beauty of Christianity lies in the assurance of the world beyond this one where there will be no pain or suffering or loneliness.

This hope for the after-life was expressed to me in a beautiful way by my father, shortly before his death. We were walking on a country road, talking quietly about life and its meaning. He then made a comment about eternal life that I will never forget. He said when he was a young man, the possibility of a future heavenly existence was not a matter of great value to him. He had enjoyed his youth, and the thought of life beyond the grave was like a pearl that was crusted over with scales and grime. The beauty of the pearl was assumed but not apparent or realized. But as he grew older and began to experience some of the inconvenience of aging, including a serious heart attack and assorted aches and pains, the encrustations fell from the pearl of eternal life, one by one. Then it shone more brilliantly, more prized than any other possession in his grasp.

My father has now achieved that pearl which gave such meaning to his earthly existence . . . even in the winter of his life. Thankfully, the same blessed hope is available to every one of God's children, including you and me![1]

Would you describe the physical changes that occur with the aging process?

The decline in old age is not just a sudden deterioration of all systems at the same level and at the same rate. There is an order of deterioration under normal circumstances; that is, if there is not some disease factor that changes it. This is the normal process of aging:

The first thing to be diminished is the perceptual or sensory contact with the outside world. The lens of the eye loses its ability to contract and focus, so we wear bifocals to give us both distant and close vision. Cataracts further damage clarity of vision in some cases.

The conduction of sound is lessened by a wearing away of the three little bones in the ear, so we don't hear quite as well as we did before. Higher pitches are the first to go, then we lose perception at the lower ranges of sound. The taste buds in the mouth and tongue atrophy, so nothing tastes quite as good as it did previously. There's not the joy in eating that we once had. The sense of smell is diminished, which also makes food less tasty, since much of the satisfaction in eating is actually derived from its pleasant odor. There's a dryness and hardening of the skin, which decreases the sense of touch. So all of the five senses are diminished and become less capable of detecting information and relaying it to the brain.

Later, we experience a change in motor activity, the ability to move efficiently. The first to diminish is control of fingertips, followed by less dexterity of the hand, then wrist, elbow, and shoulder. The lessening of coordination moves from the extremities inward toward the center of the body. That's why the shaky writing of an older person reveals his age.

Next, changes take place in the cardiovascular system. The fat in and around the heart forces it to work harder to accomplish the same purpose. When a person over-exerts, it requires longer to return to his normal rate of circulation. A gradual stiffening of the arteries also adds to the cardiac strain. Cholesterol collects in the arteries and constricts the flow of blood, which can lead to heart attacks, strokes, and other cardiovascular disorders. Furthermore, the autonomic nervous system no longer regulates the body's processes efficiently, exacerbating such problems as poor circulation.

Reproductive activity ceases—at about forty-five years of age in women and fifty or sixty years in men. Life no longer trusts us with its most precious gift of procreation.

To summarize, these are the major areas of change that occur in the process of aging: first, we experience perceptual deterioration, and second, the body undergoes a motor deterioration, that is, physical changes relating to movement. If life continues beyond that point, a decline in mental alertness may occur.[2]

Is it inevitable that sexual desire must diminish in the fifth, sixth, and seventh decades of life?

There is no organic basis for women or men to experience less desire as they age. The sexual appetite depends more on a state of mind and emotional attitudes than on one's chronological age. If a husband and wife see themselves as old and unattractive, they might lose interest in sex for reasons only secondary to their age. But from a physical point of view, it is a myth that menopausal men and women must be sexually apathetic.[3]

What does a woman most want from her husband in the fifth, sixth, and seventh decades of her life?

She wants and needs the same assurance of love and respect that she desired when she was younger. This is the beauty of committed love—that which is avowed to be a lifelong devotion. A man and woman can face the good and bad times together as friends and allies. By contrast, the youthful advocate of "sexual freedom" and non-involvement will enter the latter years of life with nothing to remember but a series of exploitations and broken relationships. That short-range philosophy which gets so much publicity today has a predictable dead-end down the road. Committed love is expensive, I admit, but it yields the highest returns on the investment at maturity.[4]

FINAL COMMENT

My purpose in preparing this book has been to provide
practical, "how to" advice regarding marital and sexual
problems. Moreover, I wanted to arrange the items in a format
that would be easily accessible to those with specific needs or
concerns. Having completed that assignment in the form of
questions and answers, I would like to conclude by explaining
why such a book was thought to be needed, and finally, what
philosophy underlies the recommendations expressed.

In previous centuries, adults dealt with marital and sexual
problems on their own, without the aid of professional advice
or the help of experts. Today, however, in an era of so-called
sexual "freedom," people have rushed to psychiatrists,
psychologists, educators, and even sex therapists for answers
to their questions about sex and personal relationships, both
in and out of the marriage commitment.

It is now appropriate to ask, "What has been the effect of
this professional influence?" One would expect that
Americans would be happier and healthier sexually than
those in nations not having such technical and professional
assistance. Such is not the case. Pornography, rape, sexual
deviations, homosexuality, AIDS, depression, and suicide are
the marks of this "liberated" society. We've made a mess of it.

Of course, I would not be so naive as to blame all these woes
on the bad advice of the "experts," but I believe they have
played a role in creating the problem. Why? *Because in
general, behavioral scientists have lacked confidence in the
Judeo-Christian ethic and have disregarded the wisdom of
this priceless tradition!*

It appears to me that the twentieth century has spawned a

generation of professionals who felt qualified to ignore the commonsense practices of more than 2,000 years, substituting instead their own wobbly-legged insights of the moment. Each authority, writing from his own limited experience and reflecting his own unique biases, has sold us his guesses and suppositions as though they represented Truth itself. One anthropologist, for example, wrote an incredibly gallish article in *The Saturday Evening Post*, November 1968, entitled, "We Scientists Have a Right to Play God." Dr. Edmund Leach stated,

> There can be no source for these moral judgments except the scientist himself. In traditional religion, morality was held to derive from God, but God was only credited with the authority to establish and enforce moral rules because He was also credited with supernatural powers of creation and destruction. Those powers have now been usurped by man, and he must take on the moral responsibility that goes with them.

That paragraph summarizes the many ills of our day. Arrogant men like Edmund Leach have argued God out of existence and put themselves in His exalted place. Armed with that authority, they have issued their ridiculous opinions to the public with unflinching confidence. In turn, desperate families grabbed their porous recommendations like life preservers, which often sank to the bottom, taking their passengers down with them.

These false teachings have included the notions that loving discipline is damaging, irresponsibility is healthy, religious instruction is hazardous, defiance is a valuable ventilator of anger, all authority is dangerous, and so on and on it goes. In more recent years, this humanistic perspective has become even more extreme and anti-Christian. For example, one mother told me recently that she works in a youth project which has obtained the consultative services of a certain psychologist. He has been teaching the parents of kids in the program that in order for young girls to grow up with more healthy attitudes toward sexuality, their fathers should have intercourse with them when they are twelve years of age. If you gasped at that suggestion, be assured that it shocked me also. Yet this is where moral relativism leads—this is the ultimate product of a human endeavor which accepts no standards, honors no cultural values, acknowledges no absolutes, and serves no "god" except the human mind. King Solomon wrote about such foolish efforts in Proverbs 14:12: "There is a way which *seemeth* right unto a man, but the end thereof are the ways of death" (KJV, emphasis added).

Now, admittedly, the answers to questions provided in this book also contain many suggestions and perspectives which I have not attempted to validate or prove. How do these writings differ from the unsupported recommendations of those whom I have criticized? The distinction lies in the *source* of the views being presented. The underlying principles expressed herein are not my own innovative insights which would be forgotten in a brief season or two. Instead, they originated with the inspired biblical writers who gave us the foundation for all of life. As such these principles have been handed down generation after generation to this very day. Our ancestors taught them to their children who taught them to their children, keeping the knowledge alive for posterity. Now, unfortunately, that understanding is being vigorously challenged in some circles and altogether forgotten in others.

Therefore, my purpose in preparing this book has been to verbalize the Judeo-Christian tradition and philosophy regarding family living in its many manifestations. And what is that philosophical foundation? It involves parental control of young children with love and care, a reasonable introduction to self-discipline and responsibility, parental *leadership* which seeks the best interest of the child, respect for the dignity and worth of every member of the family, sexual fidelity between husbands and wives, conformity with the moral laws of God, and it attempts to maximize the physical and mental potential of each individual from infancy forward. That is our game plan.

If the objectives cited above could be boiled at extreme temperatures until only the essential ingredients remained, these four irreducible values would survive unscathed:

1. A belief in the unestimable worth and significance of human life in all dimensions, including the unborn, the aged, the widowed, the mentally retarded, the unattractive, the physically handicapped, and every other condition in which humanness is expressed from conception to the grave.

2. An unyielding dedication to the institution of marriage as a permanent, life-long relationship, regardless of trials, sickness, financial reverses or emotional stresses that may ensue.

3. A dedication to the task of bearing and raising children,

even in a topsy-turvy world that denigrates this procreative
privilege.

4. A commitment to the ultimate purpose in living: the
attainment of eternal life through Jesus Christ our Lord,
beginning within our own families and then reaching out to a
suffering humanity that does not know of His love and
sacrifice. Compared to this overriding objective, no other
human endeavor is of any significance or meaning whatsoever.

The four corners of this Christian perspective have been under
severe assault in recent years, yet the philosophy will remain
viable for as long as mothers and fathers and children cohabit
the face of the earth. It will certainly outlive humanism and the
puny efforts of mankind to find an alternative.

NOTES

Key for book abbreviations:

DD — *Dare to Discipline,* Tyndale House Publishers, Wheaton, IL, 1970, trade paper.
EM — *Emotions: Can You Trust Them?* Regal Books, Ventura, CA, 1980.
HS — *Hide or Seek: Self-Esteem for the Child,* Fleming H. Revell Company, Old Tappan, NJ, 1979.
PA — *Preparing for Adolescence,* Vision House Publishers, Santa Ana, CA, 1978.
STTM — *Straight Talk to Men and Their Wives,* Word Books, Waco, TX, 1980.
SWC — *The Strong-Willed Child,* Tyndale House Publishers, Wheaton, IL, 1978.
WWW — *What Wives Wish Their Husbands Knew about Women,* Tyndale House Publishers, Wheaton, IL, 1975.

FF — *Focus on the Family* cassette tapes.

Section 1
Romantic Love
1. WWW 88-90
2. WWW 90, 93
3. PA 106, 107
4. WWW 99
5. WWW 102, 103
6. WWW 93, 94

Section 2
Conflict in Marriage
1. STTM 92-94
2. WWW 76, 77
3. WWW 78-80, 82
4. WWW 82-84
5. STTM 125, 126
6. WWW 163
7. STTM 110, 111
   WWW 179-181
8. STTM 106-108
9. STTM 108, 109
10. STTM 101-103
11. STTM 108-110

Section 3
The Homemaker

1. STTM 151, 152
2. WWW 153
3. STTM 152, 153
4. STTM 154, 155
5. STTM 158
6. WWW 165, 166
7. Urie Bronfen-
   brenner, "The
   Origins of
   Alienation,"
   *Scientific
   American,* August
   1974, p. 57. Quoted
   by permission.
8. STTM 87, 88
9. Copyrighted by
   Mary Bourgoin.

Section 5
**Male and Female
Uniqueness**
1. STTM 165
2. STTM 165-167
3. WWW 64
4. WWW 117, 118
5. WWW 114-116

6. *Family Life,*
   February 1971, vol.
   31, no. 2. Used by
   permission.
7. WWW 130-133

Section 6
**The Meaning of
Masculinity**
1. STTM 64, 65
2. STTM 168
3. STTM 191
4. STTM 51, 52
5. STTM 71-73
6. SWC 45
7. STTM 65, 66
8. STTM 174
9. STTM 173, 174
10. STTM 174-177, 179
11. STTM 180, 181
12. STTM 180
13. STTM 139, 140

Section 7
Adult Sexuality
1. WWW 120, 121

2. WWW 121, 122
3. WWW 116, 117
4. WWW 126, 127
5. WWW 127, 128
6. WWW 125, 126
7. WWW 129
8. WWW 124, 125
9. WWW 122, 123
10. WWW 96, 97
11. WWW 96, 98
12. STTM 117, 118
13. STTM 118, 119
14. WWW 130
15. STTM 121, 122
16. FF *The Lure of Infidelity*
17. WWW 130
18. SWC 226-230

Section 8
Homosexuality
1. HS 140
2. HS 140, 141
3. HS 141
4. *Cosmopolitan,* June 1974. Quoted by permission.
5. WWW 141, 142

Section 9
Coping with Menopause
1. *The Thirty Critical Problems* (cassette)
2. *Ibid.*
3. WWW 147, 148

4. *The Thirty Critical Problems* (cassette)
5. *Hormone Imbalance in Mid-Life* (cassette) WWW 155
6. WWW 154
7. WWW 153, 154

Section 10
Mid-Life and Beyond
1. FF *The Impact of Aging* WWW 175, 176
2. FF *The Impact of Aging*
3. WWW 129
4. WWW 176

QUESTION INDEX

GENERAL INDEX

OTHER MATERIALS FOR THE FAMILY BY DR. JAMES DOBSON

BOOKS:

1. *Dare to Discipline,* Tyndale House Publishers, 1970. (More than one million copies of this text have been sold.)
2. *The Mentally Retarded Child and His Family,* Brunner-Mazel Publishers, 1970. (This book was coedited with Dr. Richard Koch.)
3. *Hide or Seek,* Fleming H. Revell Company Publishers, 1974.
4. *What Wives Wish Their Husbands Knew about Women,* Tyndale House Publishers, 1975.
5. *The Strong-Willed Child,* Tyndale House Publishers, 1978.
6. *Preparing for Adolescence,* Vision House Publishers, 1978.
7. *Straight Talk to Men and Their Wives,* Word Publishers, 1980.
8. *Emotions: Can You Trust Them?* Regal Books, 1980.

CASSETTE TAPE RECORDINGS:

1. *Discipline. Cradle to College,* Vision House Publishers (One Way Library). This album contains six cassette tapes, focusing on various aspects of discipline.
2. *Preparing for Adolescence,* Vision House Publishers (One Way Library). This album contains six cassette tapes, designed to help the preteenager prepare for the experience to come.
3. *Preparing for Adolescence Growth Pak,* Vision House Publishers and Word Publishers. Contains six cassette tapes for preteens, two tapes for parents and teachers, a workbook, a textbook and instruction sheets.
4. *Kids Need Self-Esteem Too!* Vision House Publishers (One Way Library). This album contains six cassette tapes, and presents the ways parents and teachers can maximize self-confidence in children.
5. *What Wives Wish Their Husbands Knew about Women,* Vision House Publishers (One Way Library). This album deals with the basic content of the book by the same name although it contains speeches, radio interviews and counseling conversations.
6. *Focus on the Family,* Word Publishers. This twelve-tape album presents a panorama of topics relevant to family life, including marriage, parenthood, abortion, aging, family traditions, etc.
7. *Questions Parents Ask,* Word Publishers. This is a four-cassette album presenting more than sixty issues commonly raised by parents.
8. *30 Critical Problems Facing Today's Families,* Word Publishers. This twelve-tape album, as the name implies, is devoted to the major issues now confronting marriage and parenthood.
9. *To Be a Woman,* Word Publishers. This twelve-tape album is focused on concerns of special interest to women, including abortion, premenstrual tension, infertility, submission and widowhood.